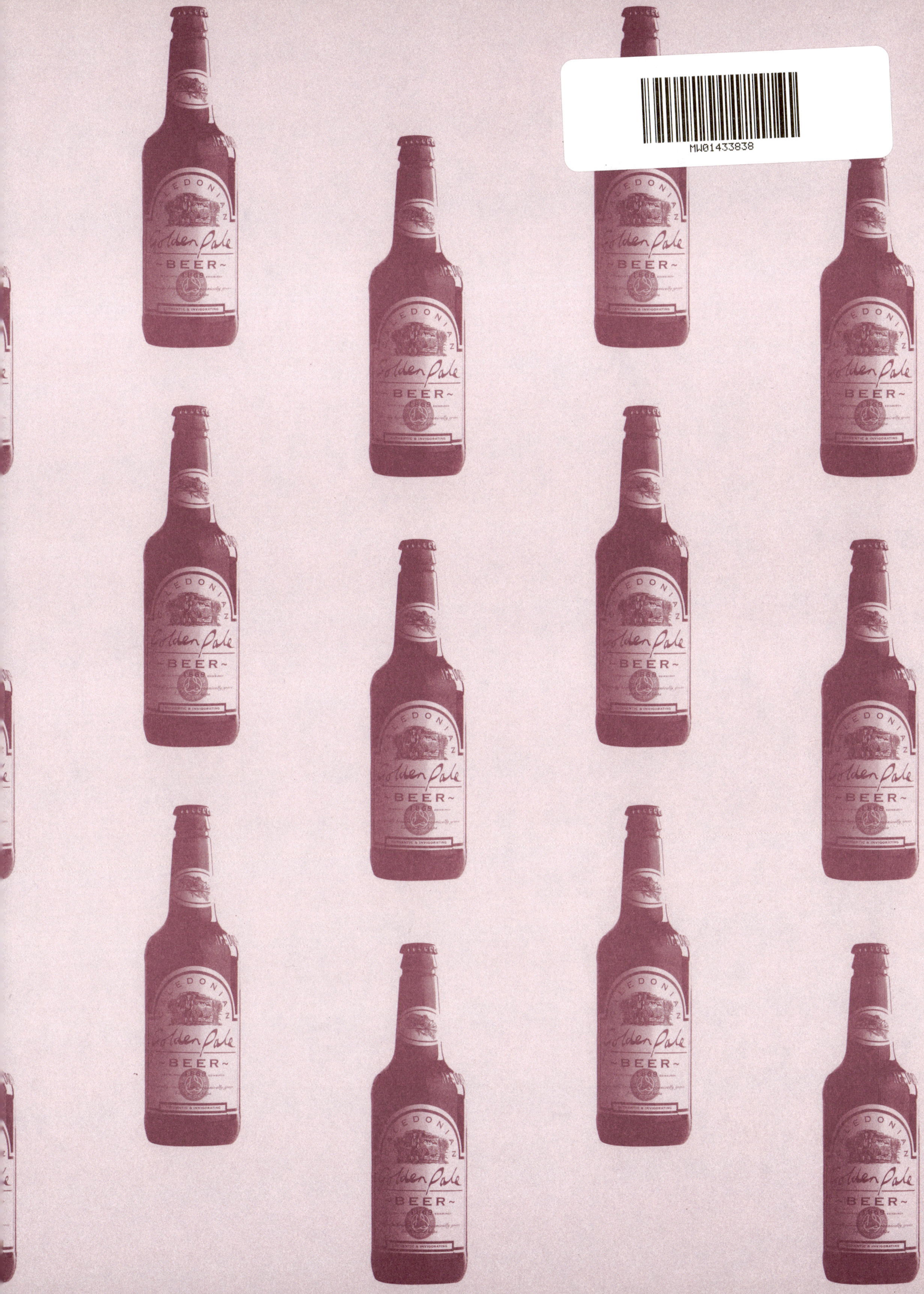
Golden Pale
BEER

The World *of*
BEER

Schöfferhofer
HEFEWEIZEN
LOWENBRÄU
PREMIUM BIER
Alc. 5,2% Vol
BREWED IN MUNICH
IMPORTED
YOUNG'S
SPECIAL
PREMIUM ALE
500 ml
250 YEARS
COBBOLD'S
250
SPECIAL
1996
MICKEYS
AMERICAN STRONG BEER
DOS EQUIS
IMPORTED BEER
PRODUCT OF MEXICO
DOS EQUIS
BEER·BIER·BIRRA·BIÈRE
CERVEZA
PETE'S
PETE'S
Wicked
Winter
Brew

The World *of* BEER

BRIAN GLOVER

HERMES HOUSE

This edition first published in 1999 by Hermes House

© Anness Publishing Limited 1999

Hermes House is an imprint of
Anness Publishing Limited
Hermes House
88–89 Blackfriars Road
London SE1 8HA

All rights reserved. No part of this publication may be reproduced, stored in a retrieval system
or transmitted in any way or by any means, electronic, mechanical, photocopying, recording
or otherwise without the prior written permission of the copyright holder.

ISBN 1-84038-215-5

A CIP catalogue record for this book is available from the British Library

Publisher: Joanna Lorenz
Project Editor: Doreen Palamartschuk
Researchers: Alison Heatherington, Daniel King
Designer: Siân Keogh, Axis Design
Photographer: David Jordan Photography

Previously published as part of a larger volume, *The World Encyclopedia of Beer.*

Printed and bound in Singapore

1 3 5 7 9 10 8 6 4 2

Acknowledgements

The publishers would like to thank the following for additional images reproduced in this book: Axiom Photographic Agency: pp22tl, 22tr, 27bl; Edifice: pp15br, 16t, 36b; ET Archive: pp8b, 9tr, 10br; Greg Evans Photo Library: pp28b, 48t; Mary Evans Picture Library: pp11tr, 14b, 27t, 35t, 39b; Fine Art Photographic Library: pp6, 13t, 19b; John Freeman: p37t; The Kobal Collection: pp16b, 21b; Peter Newark's American Pictures: pp20tc, 21t; Ann Ronan: pp8tl, 15t, 16tr, 18t, 41b, 48b; Trip Photographic Library: pp34t (photo C. Treppe); Zefa Pictures: pp26, 29t, 29b, 36tl, 39t, 40, 45t, 47b, 51t.

The publishers would also like to thank Brian Glover for images from his archive.

Contents

Introduction 6

History 8
  A Medieval Tale 12
  The Rolling Barrel 14
  Golden Transformation 16
  The Broken Barrel 18
  Concentrated Industry 22
  Consumer Revolution 24

Ingredients 26
  Water 28
  Malt 30
  Hops 34
  Yeast 38
  Other Ingredients 40

Brewing 42
  Hi-tech Brewing 46
  From Brewery to Glass 48

Styles of Beer 52

Index 64

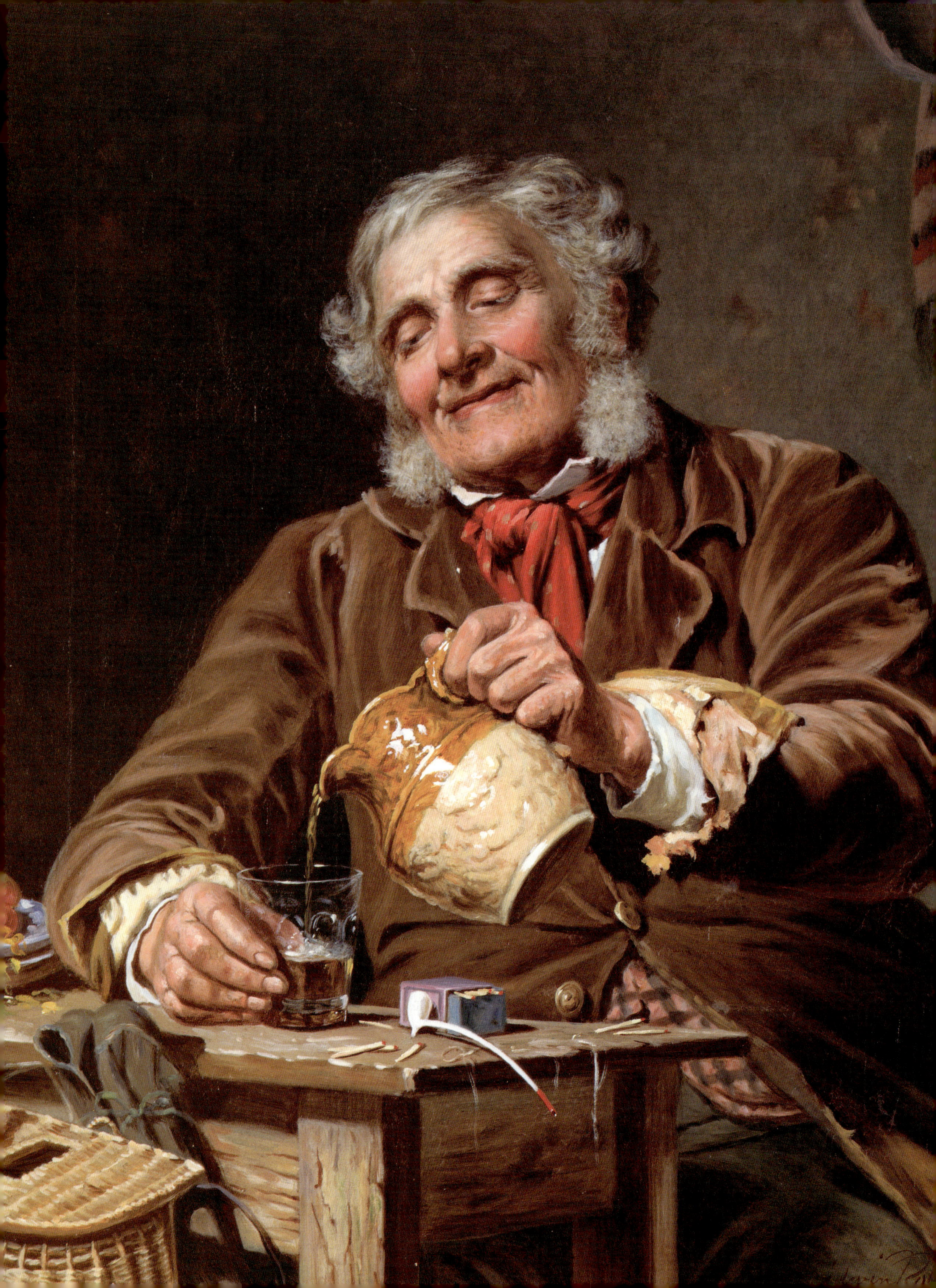

INTRODUCTION

Beer has always been the drink of the people. Malt and hops may not have inspired as many precious pens as the noble grape, but they have always provided good company. Beer is much more sociable. It is the best long drink in the world.

THERE ARE NO BARRIERS around a shared jug. "Beer cheers and heartens. It is the accompaniment of simple friendliness," said a churchman during the dark days of the Second World War. "In times such as these, people need some liquid sunshine." Beer is a most ancient drink that has had a chequered and varied history. It has been used by preachers as a religious symbol, by doctors as a medicinal treatment and by workers as a means of relaxation after a hard day's toil. Throughout the ages, in different countries beer has been both promoted as a health drink and reviled as the draught of the devil.

The brewing industry has changed fundamentally since the early medieval ale wives brewed from their kitchens, and it has been affected profoundly by the advances in technology sparked by the Industrial Revolution of the 19th century and continuing innovation of the 20th century. It has developed into one of the largest and most modern multinational industries. Beer is shipped all around the globe and large companies produce their brews thousands of miles from home. But there is still room for the small-scale producer in today's richly varied marketplace.

The huge range of beers that is drunk all over the world is dazzling, as is the variety of customs associated with it. A glass of beer does not just mean a sparkling golden lager, familiar in every land. It could be a stout or strong ale, a white beer, a wheat beer, a porter or a double bock. All are waiting to be enjoyed. This book details the history of brewing and looks at the wide range of styles encompassed by the term "beer".

Above: "Beer is Best". An advertisement from 1933 emphasizes beer's nourishing qualities.

Opposite: "A Warming Brew", from the painting by Edwin Thomas Roberts, 1840-1917.

Left: In the 19th century large breweries were appearing all around Europe. This print shows the original Salzburg premises of Josef Sigl, an Austrian brewery that is still going strong.

HISTORY

The origins of beer are lost somewhere in the mists of time but, as one of the world's most ancient and satisfying drinks, it has played an important part in many of the major cultures of the past.

MANY BELIEVE that the Middle East and Egypt were the birthplace of beer. In the mid-19th century, archaeologists excavating tombs of the Pharaoh's came across whole baskets full of grain, preserved for centuries amongst the gold and other treasures. It is no surprise that an Egyptian king should carry cereal grains into his grave. He would need bread in the next world. However, the barley grains may well have been for brewing rather than baking. Many tombs since have yielded remains of beer and preserved loaves of bread as well as barley and wheat grain. Stories abound of ancient grains being sprouted thousands of years after their entombment, but unfortunately scientific analysis has shown that, although very well preserved, the grain found in the ancient tombs is no longer fertile.

Above: A statue of an Egyptian brewer pressing out fermented bread in a basket. The "beer" drains into the jar beneath.

Below: The King of Ur and his nobles raise their glasses at a banquet – c. 2,500 BC.

THE FIRST BREWERS

Although the great early Middle Eastern civilizations did develop brewing to a fine art, they were not the first. Though no one understood how the process of fermentation worked, it was not a difficult art to carry out, and many other brewers were making grain-based alcohol long before the pharaohs. In fact, brewing alcoholic drinks developed independently more or less the world over – the end product depending on what local crops and fruits were available.

The Africans were making their own intoxicating drinks using sorghum and millet, and the Chinese were brewing beer at the same time as the Egyptians, using more advanced techniques, though they were reliant chiefly on millet and rice. In Latin America, the Aztecs in Mexico boasted their own beer gods, and Brazilian Indians produced dark, smoky-tasting brews from manioc roots and grain roasted over hardwood fires. South American Indian women brewed chicha by chewing maize kernels, spitting them into pots, mixing the mush with water and leaving it to ferment. This ancient beer is still made in some areas today.

In 1938 a cave-dwelling near Dryden, in West Texas, yielded up the remains of an early brewery and proved that the North Americans too were brewing in their prehistory.

One belief that many of these very early brewers shared was that the beer they brewed was a gift from the gods.

A civilizing influence

Some historians even argue that beer was such an important source of nourishment, and played such an important cultural role, that when people first switched from a nomadic existence as hunter-gatherers and settled down to till the land, the bulk of the grain crop was cultivated not for food, but to brew beer. The need for intoxicating liquor may have been one of the very first civilizing influences on mankind. Beer certainly played a crucial role in ancient diet as an important source of essential amino acids and vitamins, as well as providing a social drink.

The brewing civilizations of the Middle East, however, were certainly the first to record their craft and the essential role that it played in their culture.

THE SUMERIANS AND BABYLONIANS

The first detailed mention of beer was made more than 5,000 years ago by the Sumerians, who lived in the fertile land between the Tigris and the Euphrates in the area now known as Iraq. They invented writing, and among their surviving records on clay tablets more than 20 varieties of beer are mentioned and detailed recipes that include beer as an ingredient are documented.

One type of beer called *sikaru* played a central role in the Sumerian culture. It was used to honour their gods, pay their workers and feed the sick. They believed that its heady effects were a spiritual experience.

Documented brewing methods

Sikaru was liquid bread. The Sumerians moistened and germinated cereal seeds (including emmer wheat and barley), then coarsely ground them into flour before part-baking them into small cakes. The cakes were then soaked and crumbled into large earthenware pots of water and allowed to ferment for several days. The ancient brewers used dates and honey to flavour the thick, but nourishing, drink that resulted.

The final concoction was drunk in a social

Above: A 17th-century French engraving showing Brazilian Indian women making beer by chewing grain and spitting it into a vat for fermentation.

BABYLONIAN JUSTICE

In an attempt to regulate the quality of the beer produced by the larger-scale commercial brewers, the Babylonians ruled that any brewer producing unfit beer would be drowned in their own drink.

TOP BREWING NATIONS

1	US	5,220	12	France	458
2	China	2,695	13	Netherlands	449
3	Germany	2,539	14	Australia	398
4	Japan	1,518	15	Czech Republic	392
5	Brazil	1,254	16	Venezuela	354
6	UK	1,247	17	Korea	337
7	Mexico	900	18	Belgium	323
8	Russia	539	19	Colombia	319
9	Spain	535	20	Ukraine	308
10	South Africa	497			
11	Canada	486			

(Figures for 1993 given in millions of imperial gallons.
1 million imperial gallons is equivalent to 45,460 hectolitres)

TASTES OF THE PAST

In 1989, Fritz Maytag, owner of the Anchor Brewery in the United States, decided to recreate the flavour of the early Sumerian beer from 50 centuries before. He commissioned a bakery to produce 5,000 small loaves from raw barley flour with a little roasted barley and malt. These were soaked in water at his San Francisco brewery, to make a mash. Honey and syrup of dates were added for flavouring.

"We started cooking it and it was a very eerie feeling, as though we were rubbing the magic lamp," Maytag said later. The resulting cloudy, orange-red brew, named "Ninkasi", after the Sumerian goddess of brewing, was served at a brewers' conference. Guests drank the beer from huge jugs through tubes, just as the Sumerians had done.

"It wasn't wonderful beer," admitted Mr Maytag afterwards. "But it was interesting."

In 1986, Scottish home-brew shop owner, Bruce Williams, revived the ancient art of brewing *fraoch* or heather ale. First using the small West Highland Brewery in Argyll in Scotland, and then the larger Maclay's Brewery in Alloa, Williams tested different varieties of the wild heathers that colour the highland glens purple in late summer. He now produces batches of *fraoch* each flowering season. The heather flowers and the leaves of the wild myrtle, gathered at the same time, give an acidic, peaty brew with a powerful floral bouquet.

Scottish and Newcastle Breweries in Britain produced Tutankhamun Ale at their pilot plant in Edinburgh in 1996. They used the findings of Dr Delwen Samuel, of Cambridge University's archaeology department. Her research on 3,000-year-old dried remains of beer from Tell el-Amarna and Deir el-Medina, helped them to brew a beer made from malted emmer wheat, and flavoured with coriander and juniper. The husky emmer, which had not been cultivated in Egypt for over 2,000 years, had to be grown specially in England. Only 1,000 bottles of the beer were produced. They were sold at the London department store, Harrods, for £50 a bottle, the proceeds going towards further research into ancient Egyptian beer making.

Left: Tutankhamun Ale produced in 1996 was described by tasters as fruity and spicy.

way sitting round a jar. It was sucked up through reeds to avoid the husks and other debris floating at the neck. Rich Sumerians would carry their own beer-drinking reeds, decorated in gold, for drinking from the communal pot.

This early brewing required no major buildings or equipment. A maltings, bakery and brewhouse combined, consisted of a mud or reed hut with a hole in the floor for an oven, a mat and a few earthen vessels. Two flat stones served as a mill. Making beer was a domestic operation, just like preparing food.

Later, as the civilizations of the Middle East grew more sophisticated, larger brewing operations met the needs of the army, the temples and the palaces. Excavations at Ur (now located in modern Iraq, but once part of Sumerian and later Babylonian territory) uncovered a major civic brewery, dating from sometime between 2,000 and 539 BC, during the Babylonian era.

THE BREWERS OF ANCIENT EGYPT

The Egyptians were brewing a strong beer flavoured with juniper, ginger, saffron and herbs, called *heqet* and also known by the Greek name *zythum*, from as early as 3,000 BC. An ancient papyrus gives instructions for brewing *zythum*, a stronger beer called *dizythum*, and a weak family beer called *Busa*.

In order to supply the grand courts of the pharaohs and to provide the armies of pyramid workers and the bulging population with their daily rations of alcoholic relaxation, the Egyptians also perfected the art of brewing on a large scale.

As with the Sumerians and Babylonians, beer was very important culturally. It was a most important offering to the gods, and accompanied the dead on their journey to the afterlife. It was frequently mentioned on offering lists and

Right: A tavern scene on a 2nd-century Roman relief.

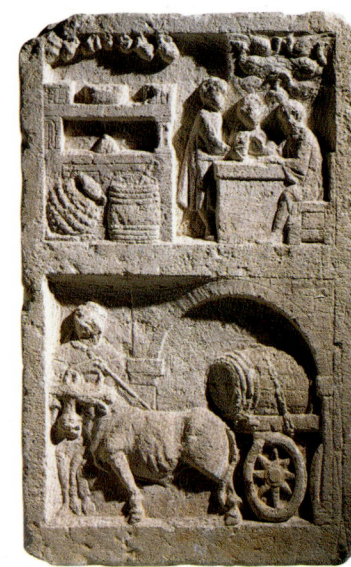

other documents, and the Egyptian Book of the Dead contains a reference to an offering of zythum at the altar. One of the Egyptians' most important gods, Osiris, was believed to be the protector of brewers.

Doctor's orders
In addition, the zythum helped the Egyptians to remain healthy. Ebers Papyrus is one of the most important surviving works on ancient medicine. It was compiled sometime between 1,550–1,070 BC from now-lost documents and word-of-mouth remedies from as far back as 4,000 BC. It contains more than 600 prescriptions and remedies, many of which rely on a beer mixture to provide cures for a variety of ailments.

The end of a tradition
The Egyptians also developed the malting process, the practice of part-baking the cereal grains, discovered earlier in Mesopotamia.

In 1990, a massive kitchen complex in Queen Nefertiti's Sun Temple was discovered at Tell el-Amarna, the birthplace of Tutankhamun. Researchers examining the remains of brewing there found that the beer had been made from an ancient strain of wheat called emmer, as well as with barley.

By the 8th century AD, however, Egypt had been invaded by Muslims. The Koran, which is the Muslim holy book, bans the drinking of alcohol, and the Egyptian brewing industry went into a decline from which it has never recovered. The knowledge of beer had already been spread far and wide. The historian Herodotus, for example, from the hot Mediterranean wine-drinking land of Greece, had travelled through Egypt in 430 BC and wrote that, "The Egyptians drink a wine which they get from barley, as they have no vines in their country."

As agricultural production of grains became more common around the world, there were plenty of other countries where grains were being grown and used for beer production.

THE NORTH-SOUTH DIVIDE
Beer brewing travelled to Europe, following the cultivation of grain. In cooler climates grapes for wine production were difficult to grow, but wheat and barley flourished. This variation in climate created something of a north-south divide in alcohol consumption.

In the 1st century AD, the Roman historian Tacitus stated that beer was the usual drink of the Germans and the Gauls, while Pliny the Elder in his *Naturalis Historia* of 77 AD, remarked that the tribes of Western Europe made "an intoxicating drink from corn steeped in water". In contrast, in the Mediterranean areas of Europe the vine reigned supreme.

The Norsemen of the far north had a culture swimming in beer. They had a tradition of feasts of celebration, where the party was kept going with copious quantities of beer drunk from ale horns, traditionally decorated with runes to ward off poisons. Ale was regarded so highly that according to Norse mythology, the warrior's resting place, Valhalla, was where Vikings slain in battle passed their days happily drinking beer.

Beer was not confined to the marauding warriors. When a young woman was buried in Jutland 3,300 years ago, she was laid to rest with a small pail at her feet containing beer. The brew, which was to sustain her in her life after death, was brewed from wheat and flavoured with bilberries, cranberries and myrtle.

Above: 19th-century archaeologists discovered baskets of grain in tombs in the Valley of the Kings in Luxor, which are believed to have been for brewing beer in the after-life.

Below: The Sumerians drank beer through straws to avoid the debris floating inside.

A MEDIEVAL TALE

By the medieval period the practice of growing grain to make beer had spread into Europe, bringing a competitor for wine – the alcoholic drink that had previously reigned supreme in some societies.

Below and right: The names of Ridleys Bishops Ale and Marston's Merrie Monk reflect the early church connection with brewing and beer.

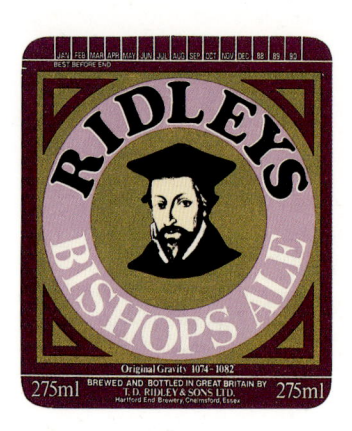

Below: Leffe Abbey, by the River Meuse in Belgium, had a brewery from the 13th century until Napoleonic times. Today beers under its name are produced by a commercial brewery.

IN MEDIEVAL TIMES, beer was more than a warming and intoxicating refreshment – it also provided a safe drink in an age when the purity of water and milk was uncertain, and drinks like tea and coffee were unknown. The process of boiling, followed by the production of alcohol, removed the main dangers of infection. The reasons were not understood, but the effects were widely welcomed.

Outside the warmer wine regions, the everyday drink was weak table beer. Stronger brews were used to celebrate the main events of the social and religious calendar. Brewers used many cereals, including wheat, rye and oats to make beer, but increasingly barley was preferred, because it was easier to malt, and produced more sugar, which then turned to alcohol. Also, in times of famine, the authorities often insisted that all the available wheat crop was used to make bread.

THE HOLY ALLIANCE

The monks across Europe helped to nurture the art of brewing during this period and their malt was especially valued. Large-scale breweries could be found in the monastic settlements that sprang up across Europe from the 5th century onwards. The monasteries supplied not only their own needs, but also those of thirsty travellers and pilgrims. Many secured their financial stability through the sale of ale outside the walls. In the 9th century, the abbey of St Gallen in Switzerland, for example, boasted its own maltings, a mill and three brewhouses, each containing a large copper cauldron heated by an open fire, a cooler and fermenting tun. Each brewhouse may have been used to brew a different quality ale – *prima melior* for the fathers and distinguished guests; *secunda* for lay brothers and other workers; and *tertia* for passing travellers and local visitors.

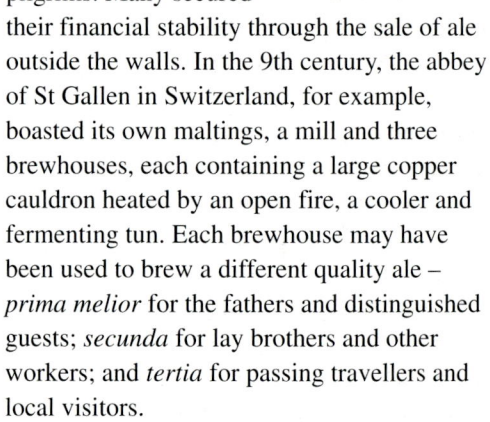

Though its use in the communion was later forbidden, the early church looked kindly on ale, regarding it as a blessing from God. An early name for yeast was "God is good", and its action was regarded as a minor miracle. Many saints, such as St Florian in Bavaria, were credited with looking after brewers.

The monks' legacy
Monasteries were so central to the development of brewing in England that the industry adopted the monks' method of marking the strength of beer – with crosses on the barrels.

Monasteries in Belgium, the Netherlands and Germany still brew beer. Some, such as the Abbaye de Notre-Dame de Scourmont in Belgium, which sells its famous Chimay ales all over the world, brew on a surprisingly large commercial scale.

Holy communities in central Europe are also credited as having been the first to brew with hops. Hops were introduced not so much for their flavour – many drinkers did not welcome the bitter taste – but for their preservative value. There are references to abbey hop gardens in the Hallertau district of Germany as early as 736 AD. The records of the Bishopric of Freising in Bavaria mention the cultivation of hops in the 9th century. In 1079, a leading herbalist, Abbess Hildegard of St Ruprechtsberg, near Bingen, wrote that the climbing plant "when put in ale, stops putrefaction and lends longer durability".

Before the hop gained ascendancy, a mixture known as gruit was added to the brew. This typically consisted of herbs, such as bog-myrtle, rosemary and yarrow. More expensive spices were used to flavour stronger ales: cinnamon, cloves, ginger, or even garlic and pepper. The heavier spices also helped to mask off-flavours and the taste of sour ale.

Lager arrives
The monks of Bavaria were responsible for an innovation that was to change the face of beer brewing – bottom-fermentation.

During the hot months of summer, fermentation was likely to run out of control and bacteria could spoil the drink. The problem was so great that in Germany in 1533, Prince Maximilian I ordained that anyone wishing to brew between April 23 and September 29 had to obtain special permission.

The Bavarian monasteries first attempted to store beer for long periods in cool cellars. This storage method caused some yeasts to change their character. At the lower temperatures, instead of frothing to the top of the fermentation vessel, the yeasts sank to the bottom and fermented much more slowly. This bottom-fermented beer could be stored for much longer periods – a process known as lagering, from the German word for storage.

Early Home Brews

Apart from the larger-scale brewing of the church, most beer drunk was brewed in the home. Brewing was a domestic chore, along with cooking and cleaning, and was dominated by women. In medieval Britain, most ale was produced at home by women known as "ale wives". In parts of northern Germany, brewing utensils were a vital part of a young woman's dowry until the 16th century.

The more successful home-brewers attracted people to their houses. As a natural consequence, their dwellings became the social centres (public houses) of their community.

As villages grew into towns, some families concentrated on brewing, and sold ale to the public and to other pubs and taverns.

Above: A monastic master brewer takes a well earned rest in "The Brewmaster's Break" by Eduard Grutzer, 1846–1925.

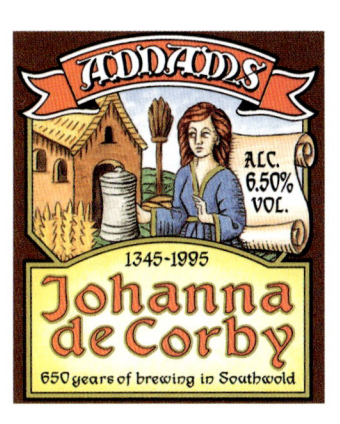

Above: Adnams brewery celebrates a notorious early English ale wife with a special beer. Apparently she was often in trouble for selling poor beer.

THE ROLLING BARREL

As the Industrial Revolution swept Europe, the brewing industry rose to meet the thirsts of the new industrial workers, harnessing the new innovations and discoveries to large-scale production.

Below: In medieval times barrels of beer would be carried short distances by hand, slung on poles.

Below: Barrels of beer being delivered by horse and cart for the 1906 Munich Oktoberfest.

By the 16th century, brewing was a well-established local craft, and most beer was still brewed at home, either for domestic consumption or for sale to neighbours. Breweries that rolled out barrels for sale chiefly supplied their own beerhouse and the local outlets they could reach easily; few went much further afield. In an age when even the best roads were rutted and pot-holed, and the only real means of transport on land was the horse and cart, there was little purpose in transporting heavy casks of beer.

Beer is a bulky product of relatively low value; brewers found that it was much easier and more cost efficient simply to brew it on the spot where it was to be consumed. Only in major cities, where there was a large market close at hand, could brewing plants grow to any reasonable size.

Beer's raw ingredients, however, were lighter and easier to handle before the water was added. As a consequence, hops, barley and malt were traded over long distances and malting (roasting part-germinated barley and other grains) rather than brewing became a major industry first. Malt was of high enough value and light enough to mean that it could be transported economically over relatively long distances. The fact that taxes were generally levied on malt rather than beer indicates the malting industry's dominant position. The prosperous maltsters tended to look down on the humble small-scale brewers that they supplied.

HISTORY

Left: The development of railways throughout the world at the end of the 19th century meant that beer could readily be transported across continents for the first time.

Above: Fäffer beer from the Lederer Brewery, Nuremberg. This beer mat shows beer barrels being carried to the waiting train.

THE INDUSTRIAL REVOLUTION

Brewing on a large scale can only flourish where there is easy access to transport. Many breweries were established alongside rivers. This was not for water supply, but to allow boats to collect the beer for transporting further afield. Many of the large London breweries, for example, supplied a thirsty market in the Netherlands and northern Germany during the 16th century. However, it was not until the development of canal transport in the 18th century, then the spread of the railways across the world in the mid-19th century, that large casks could be moved more easily than had previously been possible, and brewing, at last, was able to develop into a global business.

The power of steam

Brewing had changed little over the centuries. An ale wife from the year 1400 would have had little difficulty in recognizing the basic equipment and techniques used in 1750. Perhaps the dominance of the hop as an ingredient and the scale of the operation would have seemed surprising, but little else. All the power came from men's arms. The only steam rose from the boiling wort.

Above: Bass celebrates the arrival of steam power in the brewing industry.

However, in 1774 Scotsman James Watt patented a steam engine, and the leading brewing companies in London soon embraced this new mechanical age. Whitbread installed a Boulton and Watt steam engine in its Chiswell Street brewery in London in 1785, to grind malt and pump water. The engine made 24 horses redundant, and it was considered such a wonder that King George III visited to see the steaming mechanical marvel for himself.

The large breweries were also quick to pioneer other scientific innovations such as thermometers, hydrometers, attemperators and mechanical mashing rakes. Many of the leading names of the British and Irish industries date from the second half of the 18th century, among them William Younger of Edinburgh (1749), Arthur Guinness of Dublin (1759) and William Bass of Burton (1777).

In 1796, the Whitbread brewery in London became the first in the world to produce 200,000 barrels in a year.

The combined power of the new technology and the steam locomotive railways ushered in the era of the international brewing companies. The Industrial Revolution had transformed brewing from a predominantly local trade into a major industry.

Below: A barge on the Polntcysllte Aquaduct, Wales. The growing canal network enabled brewers to market their beer more widely.

15

GOLDEN TRANSFORMATION

The 19th century was a period of spectacular change in the brewing industry. One innovation – a mere change in colour – was eventually to alter the way the world thinks of beer.

IN EUROPE the monks' great innovation of bottom-fermented beers had caught on. However, the 19th-century brewer still worked hard to control the beer's strength and temperature during brewing.

In 1836 Gabriel Sedlmayr took over the running of the Spaten Brewery in Munich and developed the art of producing more stable, bottom-fermented beers through cold storage (the German name for which is lagering).

Despite their novel brewing method, however, these new lagered beers remained a fairly conventional dark brown or amber-red colour, like other types of beer, until 1842. It was another part of the Austro-Hungarian Empire that made the clear, golden breakthrough.

SPARKLING ACCIDENT

After yet another disastrous brew was poured down the drain in 1838, the inhabitants of the Bohemian town of Plzen (later part of the Czech Republic) decided enough was enough and built a new brewery. They then employed a Bavarian brewer named Josef Groll to brew their beer using the more reliable bottom-fermentation method.

On October 5 1842 Josef Groll mashed his first batch of beer in Plzen and the world's first ever golden-coloured lager was born.

The pale colour was probably nothing more than an accident. The barley that was grown locally happened to be low in protein, which would have helped clarity. In addition, the water in the Bubenc district of Plzen where the brewery was sited was also very soft – it contained little limestone, which tends to draw colour from the malt into the beer, so the colour remained in the malt and the beer remained pale and clear.

Above: Lager was not always a pale golden hue. For many years it was dark brown or amber-red, like most other beers.

Standing out from the crowd

In another age, in another place, perhaps no one would have noticed the sparkling, golden colour of Josef Groll's brew. But Bohemia was also famous for another industry at that time – glass making. Previously beer had been served in tankards made from wood, pottery, stoneware, various metals, and even leather. The clarity and colour of the beer didn't really matter, as long as the aroma and taste were good. But as mass-produced glass started to appear, so Plzen's sparkling golden lager stood out and began to gain popularity.

Popular pils

At the time the town of Plzen was better known by its German name of Pilsen. Soon, what came to be known as the Pilsner style began to be copied across Germany, Europe, and around the world, where they were often called pils, after their town of origin. Although some excellent Pilsners are brewed in other countries, most lagers have simply used this style as the basis for a much blander approximation of the style. Countries that had little or no brewing tradition of their own have since adopted this universally popular golden brew and Pilsner-inspired lagers have become the most widely brewed international beer.

KEEPING IT COOL

Good transport and a source of cheap mechanical power took a lot of the hard work out of the brewing process; however, these did not prove a solution to the brewers' age-old battle with the temperature. The more reliable technique of bottom-fermentation went some way towards reducing the problem of brews souring and yeast multiplication running out of control.

But the temperature of beer was becoming increasingly important, both in the bar and at the brewery. Brewers wanted to be able to brew all year round without warmer weather spoiling the brew, and beer drinkers increasingly demanded an ice-cold, thirst-quenching draught.

HISTORY

Above: Before refrigeration, ice was collected in winter and stored in underground chambers in ice houses, where it would last all summer.

A chilling breakthrough

One writer has described the 19th century as the "Century of Refrigeration". Initially, improved transport allowed greater use of ice from the lakes and mountains. Huge blocks, used on a prodigious scale, helped to keep beer cool during the summer. In the brewing city of Strasbourg, France, in 1867, there were 46 large cold stores. In the US in 1875, breweries used an estimated 30 million tons of ice.

But the technological breakthrough that freed brewers to produce their beer any time and anywhere was the advent of mechanical refrigeration. Not surprisingly, one of its pioneers came from the hot climate of Australia. James Harrison of Geelong, Victoria, developed a compression machine in the 1850s, which was used for storing many perishable products.

A problem solved

The large brewers were quick to take advantage of this breakthough. In 1870, Guinness of Dublin installed four refrigerating sets in its St James's brewery. In 1873 the Spaten brewery in Munich introduced a refrigeration plant.

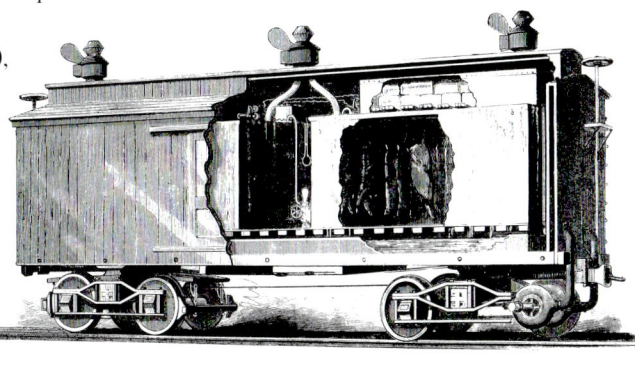

Refrigeration took over the industry. In the late 1870s, Anheuser-Busch in North America launched the first fleet of refrigerated railway freight wagons for transporting its goods from coast to coast, and by 1908, the Linde refrigeration company had supplied 2,600 machines, more than half to brewing companies. The concept of ice-cold, pale lager had arrived.

Below: The advent of the refrigerated rail car allowed the transport of many perishable goods, such as meat and beer.

Below: The idea of a cold, golden lager, born in the 19th century, has persisted into the 20th. In the film "Ice Cold in Alex", the cold beer at the end of their desert trek keeps the heroes struggling ever onwards.

HISTORY

THE BROKEN BARREL

Prohibition spelled the end of beer's rising fortunes around the developed world, as a sweep of puritanical fervour knocked the stuffing out of the prospering brewing industry.

Right: Tea drinking spread from Asia – where the samovar was a convivial focus – into Europe, where it provided a safe and sober alternative to beer.

Below: When he was Chancellor of the Exchequer, David Lloyd George introduced draconian restrictions against drink in 1915.

THE GROWING RANKS of industrial workers who, despite appalling conditions in the factories, were still more affluent than their country cousins, found comfort in cheap and powerful beer.

Public bars sprang up in the cities and drunkenness spread, as people rolled and stumbled down the streets. But by the start of the 19th century, there was, at last, a safe, alternative drink to beer. Tea and coffee were proving popular in continental Europe and North America. For the first time, beer was no longer a vital part of the everyday diet.

THE DEMON DRINK

Religious leaders were appalled by the social evil of drunkenness. Temperance preachers, raging against the evils of drink, found a swelling audience. Across Europe, campaigners against alcohol held rallies, addressed meetings and argued strongly for restrictive legislation. The gospel and the glass no longer went hand in hand.

The church was particularly keen to outlaw drinking on the Lord's Day. Calvinist Scotland – despite boasting a thriving brewing industry in Edinburgh, Glasgow and Alloa – forced through the Forbes-Mackenzie Act in 1853, introducing Sunday closing of pubs. In 1878 the Irish followed, and in 1881 Wales obtained its own Sunday Closing Act. Brewers were furious, not so much because of the trade they lost on one day a week, but because of the implied threat to their whole industry. They feared the advent of full-scale Prohibition.

The enemy within

During the First World War, the Defence of the Realm Act of 1915 slashed the number of hours that British pubs could open. The State took over breweries in sensitive areas, such as the munitions manufacturing town of Carlisle, and it closed some down altogether. Only the fear of a workers' revolt prevented the wartime government from banning the sale and consumption of alcohol outright.

When he became British Prime Minister in 1916, David Lloyd George went as far as to claim that, "Drink is doing us more damage in the war than all of the German submarines put together."

A worldwide trend

Some countries did not shrink from the drastic step of a total ban. In Canada, for example, the province of New Brunswick had prohibited the sale of intoxicants as early as 1855, and later, local option laws allowed many communities to go dry. By 1898, 603 out of 933 municipalities in Quebec operated a ban on drink. Canada introduced national Prohibition in 1918. New Zealand and Australia also teetered on the brink, as did the Scandinavian countries of Denmark, Norway and Sweden. Finland had applied Prohibition from the start of the war, even though its law did not come into effect until 1919. Iceland too froze the liquor trade in 1915. Many nations, while not banning alcohol entirely, restricted the sale of spirits, including beer-loving Belgium.

PROHIBITION IN THE UNITED STATES

The seeds of a future conflict over the issue of alcohol were sown in the very first colonies in America, among settlers arriving on the eastern seaboard of New England.

When the British sailed into North America, they brought a love of beer with them. Two years after establishing a settlement at Jamestown in Virginia in 1607, the settlers advertised in England for brewers to join them and quench the population's thirst.

At the same time, many of the new arrivals also brought a strong streak of Puritanism. The Pilgrim Fathers arrived in Massachusetts 13 years later, to escape persecution in Europe, and founded communities based on strict moral principles. For some, this religious code meant no alcohol.

The golden age of US brewing

At first this tension was hidden beneath the respectable head on the new nation's beer. President George Washington insisted that beer was provided for his troops during the War of Independence and Thomas Jefferson brewed on his Virginia estate. James Madison was eager to encourage American brewing and so in 1789 he introduced a Bill in Congress to tax imported beers.

In the New York area, British, Irish and Dutch immigrants brewed beer as they had in Europe. This practice was reinforced from the 1840s onwards by the arrival of waves of German immigrants who introduced their own styles of beer, and founded most of the US's leading commercial breweries – from New York to Milwaukee and St Louis.

During the second half of the 19th century thousands of breweries produced a wide spectrum of beers, from Pilsners to porters. In 1890, Philadelphia alone boasted 94 breweries.

Forces against drunkenness

However, the flood of immigrants from many nations, many extremely poor, also brought widespread social problems. Some drowned their sorrows when dreams of good fortune failed in the "Promised Land". Drunkenness became a major problem, and temperance campaigners began to find converts.

Reverend Lyman Beecher, a Presbyterian minister, founded the American Temperance Union in 1826, which initially objected only to strong spirits, but ten years later opposed all intoxicants. It set up organizations in every state to fight for laws banning the production and sale of alcohol.

Local law

In 1833, the Supreme Court ruled that states were free to regulate the liquor trade within their borders. In 1851 Maine passed the first Prohibition law. "The glorious Maine law was a square and grand blow right between the horns of the devil," exulted Lyman Beecher. Inspired by Maine's example, 13 more states introduced Prohibition before the Civil War bloodily intervened.

The Temperance Union, founded in 1874, was highly vocal and influential. Between 1912 and 1919, 27 states had adopted local Prohibition. One prominent member, Mrs Rutherford B. Hayes, the wife of the 19th US President, banned drink at the White House and was christened "Lemonade Lucy" by her husband's political opponents.

Above: Temperance campaigners sought to provide more wholesome alternatives to the demon drink.

Below: Drunkenness was a social problem in many countries at the beginning of the 19th century. Irish shebeens were notorious drinking dens.

History

Right: People came up with ingenious methods of hiding bottles in an attempt to avoid the Prohibition laws.

Below: Prohibition was a popular theme for movies. This poster advertises a Warner Brothers gangster movie of 1939, starring James Cagney.

National Prohibition

The 65th US Congress of 1917 was dedicated to putting the nation on a war footing against Germany. Prohibitionists took advantage of a proposal to control food production to insert a clause outlawing the manufacture of alcohol in order to conserve grain. Soon, additional wartime rulings temporarily banned the sale of all alcohol. The wet cause was not helped by rumours that the country's brewers, who were mainly of German descent, were trying to undermine the American war effort through strong beer.

The 18th Amendment shot rapidly through the House of Representatives. The end of the war brought no respite. On January 16 1919, national Prohibition of the sale and manufacture of alcohol was adopted. To enforce the amendment, Representative Andrew Volstead of Minnesota introduced the National Prohibition Act. Shops, bars, hotels and restaurants that were found selling intoxicating liquors were to be shut down and the manufacture of all liquors (anything containing more than 0.5% alcohol) was banned. The Volstead Act passed both houses in record time and came into effect on January 17 1920.

The Roaring Twenties

The history of much of the 20th century rests on the belief that what the United States does today, the rest of the world does tomorrow. Many expected Prohibition to blaze a trail across the globe. Drink seemed to be in retreat everywhere.

There was just one problem. The laws were widely evaded. What was worse, Prohibition in the United States encouraged a whole new criminal culture built around smuggling and selling hard liquor and beer, and tacitly supported by a large section of the population. Illicit manufacture of alcoholic drinks was rife. New York, which had 15,000 bars before Prohibition, soon concealed an estimated 32,000 undercover drinking dens known as speakeasies. The United States appeared to be a country ruled by gangsters and guns. The most famous American was the ruthless bootlegger Al Capone, while the St Valentine's Day Massacre in Chicago in 1929 became one of the most notorious events of the decade. The bloody massacre, when one gang of bootleggers machine-gunned another, triggered the beginning of the end for the dry era.

Pressure to repeal

Prohibition was causing a complete breakdown in law and order, and public opinion turned against it. Franklin D. Roosevelt pledged to repeal the 18th Amendment in 1932 and was duly elected President.

The 21st Amendment, ratified on December 5 1933, allowed states to make their own liquor laws. Beer could

Left: Herbert Chase was the first drunk to be arrested in New York City after the repeal of Prohibition.

flow freely again – but not in the same heady market where it had once flourished.

WORLD WAR TWO

During the First World War, the British authorities had regarded alcohol as the enemy behind the lines. But during the Second World War, beer was seen as vital for maintaining morale, both at home and among the soldiers abroad. Its value was appreciated right at the top.

"Make sure that the beer – four pints a week – goes to the troops under fire before any of the parties in the rear get a drop," thundered Prime Minister Winston Churchill in a note to his Secretary of State for War in 1944, following thirsty complaints from his army in Italy. The Royal Navy even installed a brewing plant on one of its amenity ships, *HMS Menestheus*, serving the Allied forces in the Far East. This Davy Jones Brewery – "the world's only floating brewery" – produced English mild ale from distilled sea water, hop concentrate and malt extract.

On the other side of the European firing line, as the war turned against them, the Germans were forced to abandon their beer purity law, the Reinheitsgebot, and throw a variety of substances into the mash tun. One of the stranger brews was whey beer, which was made from the milky liquid left behind from making butter and cheese. Boiled up with a few hops and then fermented, it was said to produce a palatable, if ghostly, pale beer.

The conflict took its toll on breweries everywhere. A number were bombed out of business, and most in Europe were left exhausted and in need of substantial repair. The end of the war brought little relief. In the austere late 1940s, rationing of materials and restrictions on investment grew worse rather than better.

Still the battered brewers could afford to smile, for the war had completed the rout of one foe – Prohibition. The comfort of a glass of beer had sustained many through the dark days.

Above and below: "Beer away!" The RAF developed a new way of transporting casks of beer to troops at the front.

CONCENTRATED INDUSTRY

Once beer was big business, companies realized that the quickest way to grow was to buy their smaller rivals. Some companies even rolled across borders to form huge international combines.

IN THE TEN YEARS following the repeal of Prohibition, a small basketful of brands and a handful of giant companies came to dominate the revived American brewing industry.

In countries where Prohibition had not laid its withering dry hand on the brewing business, the same process of concentration was taking place too, but at a slower pace. It rolled on remorselessly around the globe. France, for example, could boast 3,543 breweries in 1905; 90 years later fewer than 20 remained.

In Britain, strict opening hours for pubs that had been imposed during the First World War and the crushing taxes levied on beer also took a heavy toll, closing many breweries. In 1900, there were 6,477 breweries, from small pub plants to large concerns. By 1939, the number was down to less than 600. At the same time, convictions for drunkenness in England and Wales fell sharply by three-quarters, from 188,877 in 1914 to 46,757 in 1937.

THE RUSH TO GROW

The larger breweries in Britain aimed to increase sales by buying up the tied estates of smaller breweries. A new generation of entrepreneurs believed that the time was right to create international brands. The Canadian Eddie Taylor successfully introduced the lager Carling's Black Label into Britain by buying 12 breweries in ten months to form Northern United Breweries. Smaller companies rushed to grow too big to swallow, and leading breweries combined to form larger firms.

Some companies went to extreme lengths to keep their pending merger deals a close secret. Representatives of three leading regional breweries in Britain – Tetley-Walker of Leeds, Ind Coope of Burton-on-Trent and Ansells of Birmingham – met high on the moors in the Peak District of Derbyshire on a freezing February day in 1961. Over a perishing cold picnic, sheltered by a stone wall, they agreed to combine. Allied Breweries was born. After a frenzy of takeovers in the 1960s, six large groups controlled the bulk of the beer trade in Britain. By 1997 only three remained.

Above: After the end of Prohibition a few big names, Budweiser among them, came to dominate the US marketplace.

Below: Guinness headquarters in Ghana – this old name is one of the new international giants, now brewing all over the world.

Above: German beers are served to Japanese holiday-makers on the Ishigaki Island resort.

Above: The vast array of beer brands from overseas, as shown in this Cambodian market stall, disguises the shrinking number of producers.

Just over 50 surviving regional breweries were left with little more than 15% of the market.

Concentration worldwide

The concentration of the beer industry is an international phenomenon. For example, two giant brewing groups, led by BSN (Kronenbourg) and Heineken, now control three-quarters of the French beer market. And in Denmark, Carlsberg accounts for that amount by itself.

Outside Europe, the picture is more extreme. In Australia, two giants – Foster's and Lion Nathan – account for 90% of the trade. In Canada, Molson and Labatt control 92% of the market.

Not all countries have rushed headlong down this rapidly narrowing path, however. In Germany, for example, a large number of small breweries have managed to survive, helped by the fact that the conservative German drinker remains firmly loyal to his local brew.

National brands have struggled to find favour in this complex, patchwork market, which maintains a rich diversity of beer styles, often helped by regional regulations. Thus Cologne is known for its golden Kölsch beer, which can only be brewed in the immediate area, while the nearby city of Düsseldorf remains true to its copper-coloured alt style.

Germany, and Belgium to an extent, are exceptions. In most countries brewing has become heavily concentrated. Even in Germany, falling demand has meant that the smaller firms are beginning to disappear. In 1996, the brewers' organization, Deutscher Brauer-Bund, warned that intensified competition would inevitably lead to concentration. One industry expert has predicted that half of Germany's breweries will have vanished by the year 2010.

Above: Carlsberg's name is well known in its home town of Copenhagen and the world over.

An international industry

Brewing is no longer a national, but an international, industry. Some breweries have sold beer beyond their borders for decades, even centuries – the Dublin-based giant Guinness, and German breweries; Beck's, St Pauli Girl of Bremen and Löwenbräu of Munich, for example. Others have established licensing agreements to have their beers brewed abroad by local breweries, sometimes setting up breweries overseas, often in partnership with local firms.

Leading beer brands are now well known across the globe.

Collecting breweriana

The marketing paraphernalia used by brewers to promote their beers has spawned a whole new international hobby – the collecting of "breweriana". Many beer magazines have regular articles on the subject, and the range of collectibles – from antique beer mats and postcards to foam skimmers and wrist watches – is vast. Collectors correspond and swap their finds over great distances – from the Czech Republic to Australia.

HISTORY

CONSUMER REVOLUTION

One group had not been consulted about the new mass market – the consumers. A revolution, sparked in Britain, spread around the world. The demand for "real" beer has stimulated the mushrooming of new breweries.

The INTERNATIONAL companies that now dominate the world beer market inevitably wanted brands that they could sell across a wide area – brews that would appeal to everyone and offend no one. Light, mildly hoppy Pilsners, such as Carlsberg and Heineken, were often the result. The emphasis was on wide acceptability, perhaps to the detriment of individuality. Distinctive local tastes were out.

A UNIVERSAL PRODUCT

By the 1960s the leading brands in the United States, such as Budweiser, Miller High Life and Pabst Blue Ribbon, were already low in malt and hop character and flavour, while high in carbonation. As far as some consumers were concerned, the beer had almost vanished. Packaging and mass marketing were all that remained.

In Britain, for example, the big six national brewers wanted draught ales that they could promote from the north of Scotland to the southern tip of England.

From the 1960s on, the giant breweries embraced pasteurization, to ensure a standard taste and a long shelf life. Traditional handpumps, and local cask beers that matured in the cellar, disappeared from bars. They were replaced by bright plastic fonts serving the new processed and pressurized keg beers. These were sweetish and gassy, pale shadows of the distinctive bitters that they replaced.

THE CONSUMER STRIKES BACK

After muttering into their glasses that draught beer was not what it used to be, a handful of British drinkers, led by journalists Michael Hardman and Graham Lees, formed the Campaign for Real Ale (CAMRA) in 1971.

Above: The trend for "light" beer with little flavour was taken to an extreme in the 1970s with the launch of Miller Lite in the US.

Real, living, ale that continues to ferment and develop its full flavour in the cask, was what the campaign was determined to revive. Its first annual meeting in 1972 was widely reported. Today the campaign boasts over 50,000 members and tries to promote the interests of all beer drinkers – striving to maintain a wide choice of tasty beers and good pubs. It also produces a newsletter, organizes festivals and campaigns for the consumer on relevant issues – from full measure pints to sensible opening hours.

Those regional breweries who had remained true to traditional beer welcomed the new strident voice of the consumer, and others

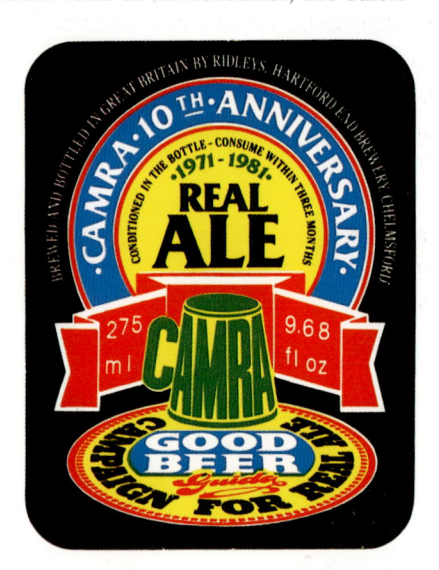

Above: CAMRA commissioned a special birthday brew from Ridleys brewery to celebrate its 10th anniversary.

began to put handpumps back on the bar to serve cask beer. Even the national brewers began to brew real ale again.

The CAMRA revolution

The CAMRA campaign was more successful than its founders could have hoped, although even they did not expect one development – the appearance of a host of new small breweries producing real ale. In Britain CAMRA's *1997 Good Beer Guide* recorded that 68 new breweries had appeared in just 12 months.

HISTORY

European initiative

The consumer revolution has taken off in Europe too. The European Beer Consumers Union (EBCU) is a blanket organization coordinating the activities of consumer pressure groups. Its members and associate members currently include the Estonian Union of Beer Clubs, the Swiss Association des Buveurs d'Orges, in Finland the FINNLIBS association, Norway's NORØL, Sweden's SÖ, OBP in Belgium, Les Amis de la Bière in France, PINT in Holland and CAMRA in the UK.

The EBCU sets out its aim as trying to help preserve European beer culture. In particular it has pledged its support for breweries that still produce high-quality traditional brews, using traditional methods.

The EBCU also campaigns against activities that are likely to lead to further concentration of control in the European brewing industry. The momentum generated by such consumer pressure shows no sign of slowing down. New breweries have appeared in almost every country – from Hungary and Romania, to Italy, France, Scandinavia and the Netherlands. Even in Germany, where many small breweries have survived, interest is stirring.

International revival

Interest in real, traditional beers has caught on throughout the world – from Canada and the West Indies to New Zealand. Experienced brewers have acted as consultants to the new breweries. British brewers, spreading the word of real ale, have even helped to start up community breweries as far afield as China.

In Australia, a former employee of the Swan Brewery in Perth, Philip Sexton, first flew the small brewery flag in 1983 at the Sail and Anchor pub in Fremantle, which developed into the larger Matilda Bay Brewing Company.

In the US, where consumer muscle has obvious weight, the revival of small breweries and a diverse range of styles have perhaps been the most extreme. In the 1970s there were only about 40 breweries in the whole vast country, but the total number of new breweries in the US is today pushing 1,000. Good beer has taken a well-deserved place in American foodie culture.

Left: Traditional bottle-conditioned ales have gained in popularity in the UK since CAMRA's activities reminded the public of their tasty qualities.

Below: Consumers have banded together all over Europe to protect their favourite tipples.

TOP BEER-DRINKING NATIONS

1	Czech Republic	155.3	11	Finland	86.1
2	Germany	138.0	12	US	85.5
3	Denmark	126.4	13	Netherlands	85.2
4	Ireland	123.0	14	Hungary	77.0
5	Austria	116.7	14	Venezuela	77.0
6	Belgium	108.1	16	Canada	68.3
7	New Zealand	102.5	17	Spain	67.0
8	UK	101.0	18	Switzerland	65.5
9	Slovenia	100.3	19	Portugal	64.1
10	Australia	97.5	20	Sweden	63.7

(1993 annual consumption in litres per head of population.
1 litre equals 1.7598 imperial pints)

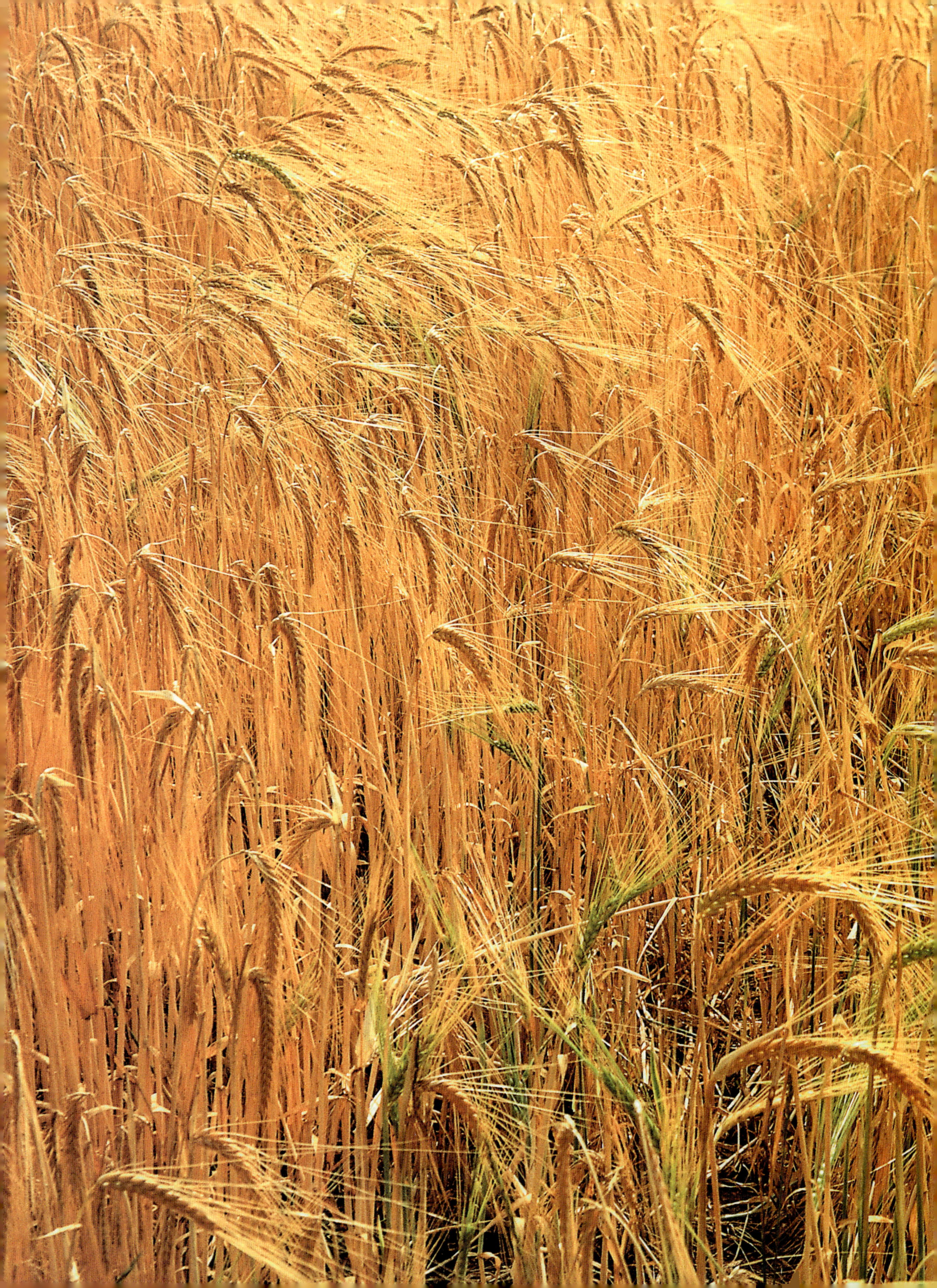

INGREDIENTS

Beer, like many things we take for granted, is little understood. It is a much more complex drink than many realize. Beer is the juice of the good earth. Its colours, from deep copper and ruby black to pale-yellow, reflect the passing of the seasons – from bare soil through to the golden harvests of barley and wheat.

THE FOAMING HEAD on a glass hides many mysteries, not least of which are beer's basic ingredients. Malt and hops feature regularly on beer labels and in promotional photographs, but how many drinkers would recognize the aromatic hop cone, one of the most unusual species in the plant kingdom? Apart from a few Belgian gourmets, nobody eats them today. Besides, how many know what malt really is? It may begin life as a waving field of cereal, but the grain has to undergo a complex series of changes – germination, roasting, and mashing – between its initial harvest and reaching the drinker's glass. There are many different types of malt. Each varies in colour, flavour and sugar content, depending upon the precise methods used to produce it. Each beer has its own "signature" combination of different malt types.

Yeast is the crucial, "magical" ingredient and its role in the transformation of the sugar in a brew to intoxicating alcohol remained a mystery for centuries. Again, there are many varieties to choose from, each with its own characteristics – its speed of action, flavour and the amount of alcohol and carbon-dioxide that it produces.

Hops are a relatively recent addition to the list of essential ingredients. The natural oils that are contained within the hop cones impart the bitterness that many drinkers demand, and help to preserve the brew. There is a mind-boggling range to choose from.

In addition to the basic ingredients, brewers sometimes add more unexpected ingredients to the recipe, such as cherries or ginger, to impart an individual flavour to their particular beer. The result of the vast number of permutations of ingredients available to the beer brewer is a mouth-watering world of choice in the global bar for the lucky beer drinker.

Above: A photograph dated 1910 shows hops being delivered to an oast-house in Kent, England.

Above left: Drip mats and labels commonly use the ingredients of beer as a motif.

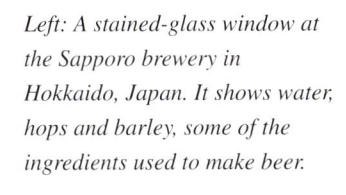

Left: A stained-glass window at the Sapporo brewery in Hokkaido, Japan. It shows water, hops and barley, some of the ingredients used to make beer.

Opposite: A golden field of barley ripening in the summer. Barley is the traditional cereal used in beer making.

Ingredients

WATER

Ask any group of drinkers what beer contains, and they may mention malt and hops. They rarely remember the greatest ingredient of all – water. Yet without a good supply, brewing good beer is impossible.

BEER IS MADE UP mainly of water, and its quality and mineral content directly affect the character of the brew. Brewers have even given water their own name – liquor.

Water contains six main component salts: bicarbonate, sodium, chloride, calcium, magnesium and sulphate. The proportions of these in the liquor used will greatly affect the flavour and sometimes the colour of the finished product. High levels of bicarbonate, for example, can produce a highly acidic mash, which will give a poor rate of sugar extraction from the malt.

Too much sulphate will produce a sharp, bitterness in the brew and magnesium is an essential nutrient for the yeast.

Many brewers like to boast about the refreshing source of the water they use to brew their beers. Hürlimann of Switzerland, for example, sells the liquor used at its Zurich brewery as a bottled mineral water under the tradename "Aqui".

In the United States, Coors of Colorado built its sales and reputation by proclaiming that its water poured from the snow-capped Rocky Mountains. To reinforce the point, a waterfall plunges from its cans and bottle labels. And in parched Australia, Tasmanian Breweries make a similar appeal with their Cascade Lager.

Some breweries have unusual water sources. Rodenbach in Belgium, famous for its sour red ales, uses underground springs to feed an ornamental lake which then supplies the West Flanders brewery, and on the parched, rocky island of Malta in the Mediterranean, where every drop of water is precious, one brewery has a rooftop reservoir in order to catch and store each brief shower of rain.

JEALOUSLY COVETED LIQUOR

A good water source was a particularly key requirement for the earliest breweries. Many of the great brewing towns sprang up around a good liquor supply. The town of Plzen in the Czech Republic, for example, had very soft water, perfect for brewing the

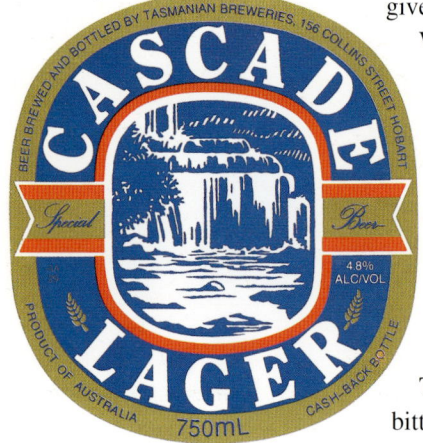

Above: The label for Cascade Lager from Tasmania uses an image of a local waterfall to emphasize the pure source of the water contained in the brew.

Below: The unique taste of Guinness was often mistakenly attributed to the River Liffey, in the heart of Dublin. In fact Guinness is brewed with water from the Grand Canal.

28

Pilsner-style lagers, and the water in Burton-on-Trent in England had exactly the right mineral content for brewing the pale ales which made the town so famous.

In England, London brewers were so jealous of the water in the small Staffordshire town of Burton that they built their own breweries there, and a Lancashire brewer miles away transported Burton water to his brewery by rail.

This fine liquid was drawn from wells sunk deep into the layer of gypsum beneath the town. Purified by slow, natural filtration, it contains high levels of trace elements of gypsum (calcium sulphate) which make for clear, bright bitters, because the calcium increases malt extraction during the mashing process. Today, breweries all over the world that want to produce pale ales usually "Burtonize" their water first by artificially adding gypsum salts.

Burton's leading independent brewer Marston's, founded in 1834, still draws more than four and a half million litres (a million gallons) each week from 14 wells, the shaft of the deepest descending nearly 300 m (1,000 ft). The family firm analyses its water daily in their laboratories, and its composition has not varied in any significant way since the company records began.

Keep Off Our Liquor!

Good water can take on mythical properties. Many Irish beer drinkers, for example, swear that the Guinness brewed in Dublin is far superior to that produced at its sister stout plant in London. They attribute the difference to the River Liffey which runs through the Irish capital. In fact, since 1868 the Guinness Brewery at St James's Gate in Dublin has taken its water from the Grand Canal which flows from St James's Well in County Kildare.

The supply of liquor to the world-famous brewery was threatened with being cut off by the Dublin Corporation in 1775. When Arthur Guinness saw that he was in danger of losing his liquor supply and potentially his livelihood, he seized a pickaxe from a workman and dared the Corporation to continue over his dead body – they backed away.

Good water is so essential for brewers that it has to be protected at all costs. So in 1994, when a concrete company planned to fill in a nearby quarry with rubbish, the Burton brewers, who feared that the scheme, would pollute their pure supply, banded together to oppose it.

More Reliable Supplies

Many breweries today have abandoned traditional wells and springs because of the threat of contamination, particularly by farmers' fertilizers. Instead, they use treated town water from the mains supply and can add the minerals that they require. It is not as romantic as a well, but it is more reliable. Breweries need vast amounts of water on tap. For every litre of beer produced, at least five more are required for cleaning and cooling.

Above: A water treatment plant may not be romantic, but it is a reliable source of good water.

Below and left: Fresh, fast flowing water straight from the Rocky Mountains of Colorado is illustrated on the Coors label.

INGREDIENTS

MALT

Malt is the body and soul of a brew. It is this partially germinated, roasted grain that provides not only the alcohol, but also much of the flavour and nearly all of the colour in a glass of beer.

Above: Barley is the grain most commonly used for malting.

Right: Oakhill's Mendip Gold label reminds us of the grain at the heart of the brew.

Below: Part-germinated grains are baked in a kiln for two days to produce the malt.

MALT IS MUCH MORE than the harvested grain. Raw ears of barley, for example, will barely ferment, and are of little use to the brewer. First they need to pass through the hands of the maltster, and in ten days a grain of barley can be turned into a grain of malt, ready to make beer. It is possible to malt other cereals besides barley: wheat, oats and rye may also be used. In fact some beer styles, such as German wheat beers, demand a wheat malt. Oats were widely used for brewing during the Second World War when barley was scarce. Barley, however, provides the best extraction rate of sugars and is therefore by far the most favoured by brewers the world over.

Barley itself comes in many forms, not all of them suitable for malting. Maltster Robert Free observed in 1888, "The art of making good malt from bad barley has not yet been found."

To produce good malt the barley must have plump, sound grains and must germinate at an even rate. It should also be low in nitrogen, as nitrogen can affect fermentation.

THE MALTSTER'S MAGIC

When batches of barley first arrive with the maltster from the field, they are screened and sieved to remove straw and dirt. Next, the barley is dried in order to reduce the moisture that it has retained, so that the harvested grain can be stored for use throughout the year. If the grain is too damp, it may go mouldy or start to germinate prematurely. Maltsters prefer to keep the barley dormant for at least a month, because this improves later germination.

Soaking the grain

In traditional floor malting, the grain is soaked in large water cisterns containing up to six tons (6.1 tonnes) of barley and 1,500 gallons (6,800 litres) of water. This steeping process takes two to three days. The barley is not kept under water the whole time. It is soaked for half a day, then the tank is drained so that the grain can breathe for between six to 12 hours before it is immersed in water again.

Germination

Next, the damp grain is emptied on to huge germinating floors, and evenly spread to a depth of 6–9 in (15–20 cm). Here it stays for five days to allow the seeds to begin to sprout and grow. This is the all-important process of germination, which turns inaccessible starches in the seeds into sugar.

The germinating grain is turned and raked regularly to ensure adequate aeration and an even growth, and to prevent the seed roots from becoming tangled together. If the workers at the maltings didn't turn the grain three times a day, you could roll it up like a coconut mat. In former times, this back-breaking work would have been done with a shovel, but today, electrically powered tools or turning machines are usually used.

Baking the green malt
After five days, when the sprouting shoots reach three-quarters the length of the grain, germination is brought to a sharp halt. The maltster does not wish to lose the newly created sugars, which the brewer will later turn to alcohol. This "green malt" is then sent to the kiln where it is baked for two days at high temperatures; the exact temperature determines the type of malt that results. Some Bavarian maltings still use wood-fired kilns, giving the malt a smoky flavour.

Nothing is wasted and the malt is screened after baking to remove the rootlets – known as "malt culms", which are sold as animal feed.

Final transformation
Once the roots are removed, the malt looks little different from the original grain. However, one bite will reveal the miraculous transformation in its flavour. The baked grains are no longer hard but good to eat, with a crunchy, nutty texture.

This delicious final product is used not only to brew beer, but also to make malted drinks, biscuits and breakfast cereals, and as an essential ingredient in malt whisky.

The Modern Industry Emerges
Traditional floor malting was the system used in most countries until well into the 20th century. The buildings can be seen in many grain-growing areas, usually alongside watercourses or railway lines. Some maltings are substantial – long and heavily built with thick walls and narrow windows, and layer upon layer of germinating floors. Some breweries once had their own maltings, larger than the brewhouse itself, but nearly all have now been converted to other uses such as a bottling hall or warehouse. Others have been demolished, turned into industrial units or converted into shopping malls.

In general, traditional floor malting, which was highly labour-intensive and seasonal, has been abandoned. As mechanization spread

Left: Wheat, oats and rye can all be used to produce brewing malt, as well as barley. Oat Malt Stout is a traditional brew from Alloa, Scotland.

Below: A combine harvester cutting a field of barley. Malting barley is subject to rigorous quality controls to ensure that it is low in nitrogen.

INGREDIENTS

Above: The Estonian Saku brewery celebrates the grain harvest on this bottle label.

Right: The Efes brewery of Turkey gets its barley from the plains of Central Anatolia and processes over 100,000 tons a year at its malting plants. Their malt is exported to breweries in South America and Africa.

Below: There are several types of malt, differing in flavour and appearance according to the precise way that the barley has been kilned.

throughout industry in the 19th century, some maltsters began to look for new methods.

A Belgian maltster named Galland developed drum malting in the 1870s. This system transferred the grain from steeping tanks into huge, airtight metal cylinders that slowly revolved to turn the grain.

About the same time, a Frenchman called Saladin introduced the efficient drying method – the "Saladin Box" system that forced air through the perforated floor of a box containing grain to the depth of 2 to 3 ft (60 cm – 1 m). This technique was later further developed in Germany into the Wanderhaufen or "moving piece" process, in which the grain slowly flows through the box.

The new systems saved space and labour, and could operate throughout the year. However, they caught on quite slowly, partly due to mechanical problems, and also because of the expense of buying new equipment. Many brewers believed that floor malting was best and indeed some still insist on traditionally made malt.

The global market

It wasn't until after the Second World War that mechanical malting methods were widely adopted, bringing in their wake even larger-scale malting plants and concentration in the industry. By the 1970s in Britain, for example, two huge companies – Associated British Maltsters (ABM) and Pauls & Sandars – had come to dominate the malting trade, accounting for more than half of all sales. Some companies operated maltings in several countries and exported far and wide.

In fact only a third of beer-making countries produce significant amounts of malt, and only eight countries supply three-quarters of the world's needs (see table). Malting depends on a reliable supply of barley. There is a huge international market – a grain-growing country such as Australia supplies its neighbours, including the Philippines. Some major brewing nations, such as Japan, have no large malting industry and the brewers there import the bulk of their requirements.

The brewers' search for a particular quality of barley resulted in an international grain market. In the 19th century, Denmark and France were regarded as excellent grain-growing countries, and barley from there was highly coveted. An area of central Europe covering Moravia, Silesia and Bohemia also developed an excellent reputation. Grain from here was known as Saale barley, and sold well, mainly through the Hamburg market. By the 1930s, brewers were competing with each other all around the globe to purchase sun-ripened crops from California, Chile and Australia.

Barley varieties

Surprisingly, much of this worldwide market was in barley that came from a few original varieties. In the 1820s, the Reverend J.B. Chevallier spotted a barley growing in an English labourer's cottage garden in Debenham, Suffolk. He was struck with the barley's extraordinary quality, and saved the

Pale malt

Crystal malt

32

seed. From that the Chevallier barley strain was developed. Archer was another popular English variety.

The barley plant produces kernels of grain which grow in either two or six rows. Chevallier and Archer are both two-rowed barleys. In the United States, six-rowed barley is preferred.

After the Second World War, Archer and its hybrids Spratt-Archer and Plumage-Archer gave way to Proctor, which was better suited to mechanized farming. Modern varieties include Triumph, Kym, Klages, Halcyon and Pipkin.

Some more traditional brewers have remained true to lower-yielding (for the farmer) but more characterful and reliable grains (for the brewer), for example Maris Otter and Golden Promise.

Types of Malt

Malt comes in a variety of styles, depending on how it is kilned. The higher the temperature, the darker the colour and more profound the flavour. The brewer skilfully blends different malts to produce different beers.

Pale malt

This is the standard malt in most beers. The barley is baked in the kiln over 48 hours with a slowly rising temperature. Pale malt is ideal for both light-coloured ales and golden Pilsners. Some specific Pilsner types are known as lager malts. Other varieties tend to be used in small amounts in conjunction with pale malt.

Amber and brown malts

This barley is heated to higher temperatures than pale malt to give more coppery colours to the brew. Amber and brown malts are rarely used today. In Continental Europe, Vienna malt provides a reddish tinge to the beer.

Global Malt Production

US	2.85
Germany	2.16
Britain	1.67
France	1.18
China	1.08
Canada	0.76
Belgium	0.76
Australia	0.64
Others	4.62
Total	15.72

(All figures in millions of tons. 1 ton = 1.016 tonnes)

Crystal malt

An exceptionally rapidly rising temperature in the kiln dries out the barley husk, leaving behind a hard, sugary, crystalline core. Crystal malt adds a fuller, sweeter flavour to beer. Dark varieties are called caramel malts; lighter ones, carapils malts.

Chocolate malt

The barley is steadily heated to about 200°C (400°F). This deep chocolate malt generates a complex mix of roasted flavours as well as a dark colour.

Black malt

Black malt is chocolate malt that has been taken almost to the burning point. Because of its powerful bitter taste, it is used sparingly, even in stouts and porters.

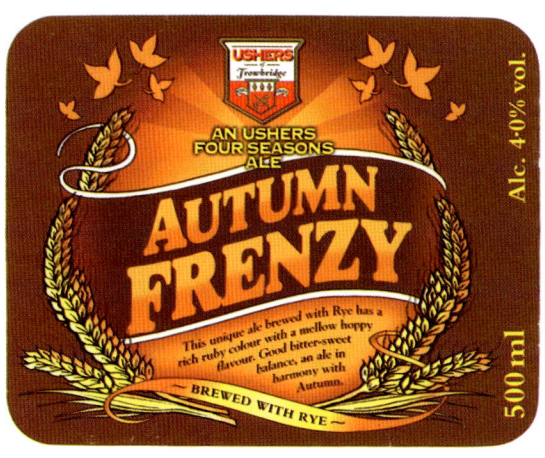

Above: Autumn Frenzy's label evokes the harvest season.

Chocolate malt

INGREDIENTS

HOPS

The cones of the hop plant were originally added to beer as a preservative. They prevent the brew from going sour, but also bring a characteristic bitter flavour and aroma to the drink.

IF MALT PROVIDES BEER with its body and colour, hops add immeasurably to its flavour by countering the cereal's sweetness with a sharp, bitter tang. The hop also gives beer its heady aroma. It is the seasoning and spice in the barley meal.

Medieval holy communities in central Europe are credited as having been the first to brew with hops. But while the monastic brewers may have welcomed the hop plant, which preserved the life of their beer, various vested interests strongly resisted its development. The powerful Archbishop of Cologne, for example, enjoyed a monopoly on the herbs used for flavouring beer and so tried to suppress the use of hops. Only in 1500 did he agree to take a rent in lieu of his rights.

In the Netherlands in the 14th century, many drinkers were developing a taste for hopped Hamburg beer from over the border in Germany, in preference to their locally brewed gruit ales. The Dutch nobility, who had vested interests in the sale of herbs, tried to exclude foreign beers or impose high import duties. But the barrel barrier failed and soon many Dutch brewers were brewing hopped beer to compete with Hamburg. In response, the Emperor Charles IV granted the nobles a tax on hops.

The hop spread from the Low Countries into England. Hopped beer was imported into Winchelsea in Sussex by 1400, and before long brewers from Flanders followed, setting up their own beer breweries, much to the disgust of the English ale makers.

Above: The type of hop used affects the flavour of the resulting beer. The Hogs Back Brewery is proud of the Goldings variety that it uses in its Traditional English Ale.

Below: Hops may be added either slightly crushed (as shown), or as condensed pellets.

Above: In the days before mechanical harvesting stilts were necessary in order to reach the cones of the tall, spindly hop vine.

Their concern was understandable, for hopped beer kept much better than the sweeter ale, especially in summer. For a while they had the backing of the authorities – Henry VIII banned the royal brewer from using hops in 1530. Nevertheless, by 1600, the use of the hop was widespread. True unhopped ale was in decline. James Howell, a Royalist imprisoned during the Civil War, wrote in 1634, "In this island, the old drink was ale, noble ale, but since beer hath hopped in amongst us, ale is thought to be much adulterated."

CULTIVATING THE HOP

The hop plant (*Humulus lupulus*) is a tall, climbing vine that is a member of the hemp family. It is distantly related to both cannabis and the nettle.

A single plant carries either male or female flowers. Only the female flowers form the vital cones required by the brewer.

The female cone is made up of a number of petal-like structures called bracts. As the cones ripen, the bases of these bracts bear glands

34

INGREDIENTS

Left: Tallying up the day's work – from a 1910 postcard. The hop harvest in Kent, England was the traditional holiday for gypsies and workers from the East End of London.

that are filled with a yellow resinous substance known as lupulin. It is this complex oil, found nowhere else in the plant kingdom, that contains the alpha acids which give the hop its characteristic bitterness.

The hop plant needs deep soil to grow, as its roots can go down for over 6 ft (2 m). It can thrive in any temperate climate, as long as there is sufficient heavy rainfall during the growing period, and plenty of sun to help the flowers ripen.

Growing at breakneck speed

Each year the plant is cut back to the rootstock, then in the spring shoots covered with hooked hairs called bines surge upwards. The hop farmer provides a support network of poles and wires for the hairy shoots to wind around and form the characteristic tall, leggy plants. Shoots can grow as much as 1 ft (35 cm) in a single day, and eventually reach 15–18 ft (5–6 m) in height.

The flowers appear in summer and are followed by the cones which are harvested in early autumn. Traditionally this was done on stilts, but today mechanization has made the task much easier.

AN ANCIENT PROFESSION

At one time, hordes of hop-pickers came from the cities to carry out the work by hand, living in tents or wooden huts on the land. For many poor families from the industrial towns, this was their annual holiday – a breath of fresh country air away from the grime and smoke. Nowadays, the labourers have been replaced by machines.

Once harvested, the hops are dried gently in kilns, then pressed into tall sacks or pockets (bales), as long as 6 ft (2 m), ready for the brewery, or for further processing. These pockets usually carry the emblem of the growing area.

HOP BY-PRODUCTS

Many traditional brewers still prefer to use whole hop cones in their recipe, but processed derivatives are commonly used today. About two-thirds of the world's hop crop is treated in some way before it is used by a brewer.

Below: Modern harvesting methods and short-growing varieties have revolutionized the previously labour-intensive business of hop picking.

35

INGREDIENTS

Above: The hop, Humulus lupulus, *is the raw ingredient which provides beer's bitter flavour.*

Below: The distinctive witch's-hat-shaped cowls, wind vanes and hot air outlets of traditional oast-houses became a characteristic feature of the landscape in hop-growing regions.

The simplest by-product is made by grinding the cones into powder, which is then pressed into pellets that are easy to transport and work well with modern equipment. However, pellets do not provide the filter bed of hops required by some older breweries.

Hop extract is another alternative. This treacle-like substance is sold in a can. It is very stable and highly efficient, but can give the beer a more cloying flavour than whole or pelleted hops.

TYPES OF HOP

Traditional aroma hop varieties give beer a subtle, fine flavour and an enticing nose. In recent decades, the emphasis has been on extracting more bitterness by developing "high-alpha" varieties.

Because many hop farms have been badly hit by fungal infections, notably Verticillium Wilt, creating disease-resistant varieties is now a research priority in many countries.

Bramling Cross
A 1920s cross between an English Golding and a Canadian wild hop. It was unpopular in the past because of its "blackcurrant" nose, but its character is more appreciated today.

Cascade
A fruity American aromatic hop first introduced in 1972.

Above: Brewers throughout the world feature hops on the labels of their beer.

Crystal
A mildly aromatic American hop.

Fuggles
Propagated by Richard Fuggle in Kent in 1875. It is also grown in Oregon, US, and Slovenia. In Slovenia it has adapted to local conditions and is known as "Styrian Goldings".

Goldings
Originated in East Kent in the 18th century. It has a flowery bouquet and is used for dry-hopping traditional English ales in the cask.

Left: At the Hop Exchange in London, England hops of many different varieties were traded from all over the world.

Hallertauer Mittelfrüh
A traditional aroma hop from the Hallertau district in Bavaria, the world's largest hop-growing area (responsible for a fifth of global production). This hop has been almost wiped out by disease.

Hersbrucker
A traditional variety from the Hersbruck hills, this has now replaced Hallertauer as the most popular German aroma hop in the brewing industry. It is grown throughout the Hallertau region in Bavaria.

Huller
Huller is a new German aromatic variety, which was developed at the Hull Research Institute in Hallertau.

Mount Hood
Based on the German Hallertauer, this American aroma hop was introduced in 1989.

Perle
Perle is a newer German aroma hop. It is also grown in America.

Progress
This Wilt-resistant hop was introduced in the 1950s in England as an alternative to Fuggle.

Quingdao da Hua
Derived from Styrian Goldings, this is the predominant Chinese hop.

Saaz
The classic aroma hop from Zatec in the Czech Republic provides just the right flowery bouquet for Bohemian Pilsners.

Select
The Hull Research Centre in Hallertau developed this new German aromatic variety.

Spalter
A traditional German variety mainly grown in the Spalt region near Nuremberg.

Styrian Goldings
Slovenia's main aromatic hop.

Tettnanger
This is a delicately aromatic German hop, mainly grown in the Tettnang region by Lake Constance on the Swiss border.

Tradition
Despite its name, Tradition is a new German hop variety.

WGV
Whitbread Goldings Variety was widely planted in the 1950s in England, as it can survive Wilt attacks.

Willamette
An American variety related to the English Fuggle, introduced in 1976.

High-alpha hop varieties

Admiral (England)
Brewers' Gold (England, Belgium and Germany)
Centennial (US)
Challenger (England, Belgium and France)
Chinook (US)
Cluster (US)
Eroica (US)
Galena (US)
Magnum (Germany)
Northdown (England)
Northern Brewer (Germany, England)
Nugget (US, Germany)
Orion (Germany)
Phoenix (England)
Pride of Ringwood (Australia)
Super Styrians (Slovenia)
Target (England, Germany and Belgium)
Yeoman (England)

INGREDIENTS

YEAST

Without yeast, malt, hops and water will never make beer. It is the catalyst that transforms the hopped cereal solution into a potent drink, hiding its magic beneath a living cloak of froth and foam.

YEASTS ARE LIVING ORGANISMS, members of the fungus family. Their scientific name is *Saccharomyces Cerevisiae*. Each yeast plant consists of a tiny, single cell, invisible to the naked eye. It is only when many millions are massed together that they become visible – as when they multiply to make beer.

The spherical yeast cells reproduce by budding. A bud forms on the parent, then, when it has grown to the same size, it separates to form another cell. Multiplying in this way, under good conditions (such as in a nutritious sugar solution) the cells can reproduce every two hours.

THE BREWER'S FRIEND

During the fermentation process, the yeast cells clump together (flocculate). In top-fermenting beers such as stout, the yeast cells rise to the surface of the liquid in the fermenting vessel. By contrast, in bottom-fermenting beers such as lagers, they sink.

The yeast gets the energy for its growth during brewing by consuming the sugar solution in the mash provided by the malt. Alcohol and carbon dioxide are the waste products of its reproduction cycle. In fact, the yeast growth and the fermentation of the brew slow down, and eventually stop, once the solution contains too much alcohol.

Many brewers use the same yeast, jealously guarded, for years. Each different strain has its own characteristics. Some work especially quickly, while others ferment to a greater degree. Each gives its own unique flavour, and particular types produce specific types of beer.

Some brewers even leave the yeast in the beer to give extra flavour; the cloudy Hefe wheat beers of Germany are classic examples of this technique.

At the end of each brew the brewer skims off some of the yeast, ready for use in the next batch. But the vast bulk is pressed, dried, and sold as nutritious yeast extract.

UNRULY ORGANISM

When yeast is working it can quickly run riot. This unpredictable organism often surprises even modern laboratories, and causes deep despair for brewers as they search for consistency.

Yeast may be a plant, but it can be a beast to control, and anyone who has seen a vigorously fermenting vat of beer, popping and heaving, will understand this fear. Yeast has a life of its own. Some brewers talk about yeast as though it were a difficult friend, and most agree that it can be awkward. Yeast can be greedy and troublesome and liable to let the brewer know if it is not being treated correctly.

SECRET LIFE

Scientists have spent many years peering through microscopes in order to uncover the workings of this secret beer agent. A Dutchman named Leeuwenhoek first described the appearance of yeast in 1685; however, it was not until Frenchman Louis Pasteur's work in the 19th century that its true role in fermentation was understood.

Below: Louis Pasteur, from the portrait by Albert Edelfelt, 1885. Pasteur, who gave his name to pasteurization, was the French scientist who discovered that yeast was a living organism.

Above: Gazing down a powerful microscope the tiny, single, living cells of the yeast fungus become clearly visible.

INGREDIENTS

LOUIS PASTEUR

French scientist Louis Pasteur is the father of modern brewing. His work on yeast allowed brewers to understand for the first time exactly what happened during fermentation. Previously, it had been almost as big a mystery at the start of the 19th century as it had been in medieval times or even in ancient Egypt. Beer frequently went off and became undrinkable, and the brewers had no idea why. Most companies expected losses of 20% or more through waste, and regularly had to destroy whole batches of sour beer.

Beer of national revenge

Pasteur was already a world-famous scientist when he started to study beer in 1871. His work was motivated by national pride in the aftermath of France's humiliating defeat by German forces in the Franco-Prussian war. He started his researches "with the determination of perfecting them and thereby benefiting a branch of industry wherein we are undoubtedly surpassed by Germany," he wrote in the preface to his ground-breaking work *Etudes sur la Bière*, published in 1876. He called his resulting brew, which he went on to patent, "Bière de la Revanche Nationale" (Beer of National Revenge).

By examining yeast through a microscope, Pasteur demonstrated that yeast was a living organism, and he was able to identify and isolate the contaminants that had been causing brewers so many problems.

His work prompted J.C. Jacobsen to build a magnificent laboratory at the Carlsberg Brewery in Copenhagen in the late 1870s, where another great scientist, Emil Hansen, was able to break yeasts down to single strains.

Hansen also showed that by isolating and using the right strain of yeast, brewers could produce dependable beers. The art of brewing was never the same again.

The main bottom-fermenting yeast, *Saccharomyces Carlsbergensis*, is named after the Danish brewery in honour of the innovative work that Hansen carried out there.

MULTIPLE STRAINS

Although pure, single yeast strains are more predictable to brew with, many brewers still prefer to use multiple yeast strains. Each reacts with the others to produce the final beer. Bass of England, for example, uses two strains, while Palm of Belgium juggles with four.

Belgian brewers of lambic beers still use wild yeasts. They rely on the natural spores of yeast carried in the air spontaneously to ferment their beer – as their ancestors did centuries before.

Left: Top-fermenting yeast boils and heaves itself to the top of the fermenting vessel.

Above: Dormant dried yeast.

Above: Ten minutes later, after water and sugar are added, the yeast is frothing and bubbling.

Handle with care

Yeast must always be handled with care. It is all too easy to break the delicate balance of multiple strains through chance infection by other microbes – or even by the introduction of new equipment. Cleanliness is vital. Even the introduction of new equipment or a change in the shape of the fermentation vessel can alter the characteristics of the yeast, and therefore the taste of the beer.

Left: The Carlsberg brewery, where Emil Hansen carried out his ground-breaking research on brewing yeasts.

OTHER INGREDIENTS

Although the basic four ingredients – water, malt, hops and yeast – are all that you need to brew beer, many brewers add other substances to their recipe, perhaps to produce a distinctive flavour and aroma, or simply to save money.

A BREWER IS NOT RESTRICTED to the four main ingredients. There are as many recipes and potential ingredients as there are brews. As well as the great variety to be found within malt, hops and different water compositions, there are also many extra ingredients that can be added to the brew to produce a highly individual recipe. As a result, flavours can vary enormously even within one beer type. As well as flavour variations, however, there are other reasons for including additional ingredients in the brew – to reduce costs or to improve the colour, for example.

Below and right: Kriek is a traditional Belgian recipe that includes cherries in the brew to produce a tart, fruit-flavoured, red beer.

ADJUNCTS
Some brewers add other substances to the mash besides malt. These "adjuncts" are added to the grist, when the malt is cracked in the mill. Adjuncts can be used to provide a cheaper substitute for part of the malt, or when malt is in short supply. Sometimes, however, the extra ingredients can simply be added to enhance the flavour of the beer. Light beers in particular tend to use additional unconventional grains in their mash. Brewers who spurn the temptation of using adjuncts boast that they produce "all-malt" beers.

Sugar
The most common adjunct is sugar, in blocks or as syrup. It ferments easily and quickly to give more alcohol, but leaves little in the way of body. Heated sugars or caramels are sometimes used instead of coloured malts to darken beers. Belgian brewers often use a less-refined candy sugar. This adjunct is particularly favoured in Africa, where barley is scarce. For example, sucrose is one of the main ingredients in Castle Lager from South African Breweries.

Flaked maize
Maize (corn), usually processed into flakes, is widely used. In some American breweries it accounts for as much as half the mash, giving a very dry, light-coloured beer.

Rice
Rice, like maize, can be a partial alternative to malt. The world's best-selling beer, Budweiser, from Anheuser-Busch of the US, uses rice to give a clean, crisp finish.

INGREDIENTS

Torrefied wheat
This heated cereal, or popcorn, is added to help head retention.

Malt extracts
Malt syrups are sometimes used to make a larger brew than the capacity of the mash tun allows. They are also popular in home-brew kits, since using extract allows the home brewer to miss out the process of mashing altogether.

Roasted barley
Unmalted roasted barley is sometimes used to blacken brews. It gives a harsh, dry flavour. The classic Irish stout Guinness uses a small amount of roasted barley in the mash to give the beer its distinctive bitter flavour.

FLAVOUR ENHANCERS

Adding extra flavourings in beer is an old tradition. In the days before the hop, brewers made their own flavouring called gruit. The recipe for each brewer's mix was a secret but it would often contain herbs, spices or fruit, such as juniper or bog-myrtle. In some countries the tradition of adding extra ingredients for flavour died out, but some brewers clung on to their tradition and the Belgian brewers, for example, never gave up their age-old fruit beers. With the revival of small-scale breweries, unusual flavourings are also making a comeback.

Honey
Honey is one of the oldest flavour enhancers known to man, and it has been used in cooking and in drink making for centuries.

Chilli
Beers with whole chillies in the bottle are a relatively new innovation, presumably a follow-on from the craze for Mexican lagers in the 1980s. It is an unusual taste sensation.

Spices
Ginger beer is a familiar non-alcoholic relic from prohibition. However, ginger is also used to flavour alcoholic beer.

Herbs
Adding herbs such as coriander to flavour the brew is an ancient tradition that has been revived by Hoegaarden.

Fruit
Orange and lemon peel, apples, raspberries, cherries and bananas have all been added to beer with various degrees of success. Some of the newer fruit-flavoured brews were conceived by modern marketing departments and often use fruit juice or extract simply as a flavouring. However, some traditional recipes use the fruit to spark a natural secondary fermentation as well as to add flavour. Two ancient Belgian recipes, Kriek and Frambozen, use cherries and raspberries.

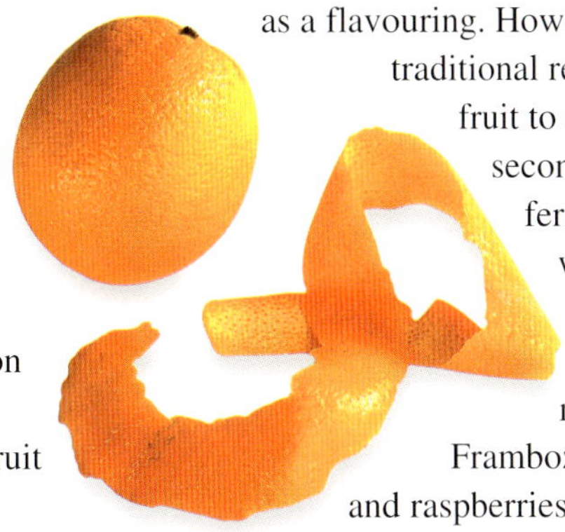

ADULTERANTS

Unscrupulous brewers seeking to maximize their profits by using inferior ingredients in the brew have long been a problem that the authorities have tried to legislate against for centuries. One common illegal additive in the 19th century was salt, which was used to "bob" the beer – to make two or three casks from one good one. It is shown here in the *Illustrated London News* in 1850, being added to the brew in blocks. Other common substances used to make the beer go further were treacle and water.

Below: Hoegaarden is spiced with coriander seeds and curaçao orange peel.

BREWING

The basics of brewing are little changed since the time when it was a domestic chore like baking. The vessels may be larger and more complicated, but the principles remain the same.

ONCE THE MALTED CEREAL has been delivered by the maltster and the hops have arrived, either in pellets or as whole dried cones, the brewer is ready to begin one of the oldest crafts in the world. It doesn't matter whether brewing is carried out in an enormous city plant or in a tiny back room behind a tavern or bar, the basic processes that are involved remain the same.

EXTRACTING THE SUGARS

The first step in making beer is to extract the sugars that are stored up in the malt, no matter whether it is malted barley, wheat or any other grain. The malted grain is ground in a mill. The crushed malt is known as grist. The grist is then mixed with hot liquor (the brewer's term for water) to produce a sweet-smelling mash that looks rather like porridge and is left to settle in a vessel known as a mash tun. There are two methods of extracting the sugars from the malt: infusion and decoction.

Infusion

The hot liquor is left to dissolve the sugars in the crushed malt until, after a couple of hours, the mash tun contains a warm, thick, sweet liquid called sweet wort and the remaining soaked cereal. The sweet wort is then drained away through slotted plates in the base of the mash tun. The soaked cereal that is left behind is sprayed (sparged) with more hot liquor to wring out any final sugars lingering in the malted grain. The spent grain by-product is then sold as cattle feed.

This relatively simple system is most commonly used in ale brewing.

Decoction

In the more complex decoction system that is usually used for bottom-fermenting beers, such as Pilsner beers, the mash is drawn off (decocted) from the tun little by little at different stages. Each part is passed to a cooking vessel called a mash cooker, where it is slowly brought to the boil, in some cases through precisely controlled temperature steps.

After a few minutes at boiling point the wort is then returned to the mash tun. The aim of the decoction process is to extract as much sugar from the malt as possible by mashing in various temperature steps. This is particularly important in lager brewing because lighter malts, which contain less sugar, are used. Brewers seek to maximize the rate of sugar extraction from the malt by drawing off twice (double decoction) or even three times (triple decoction) over a period of a few hours.

The decoction method is usually used in conjunction with another filter vessel, the lauter tun. The lauter tun contains rotating knives or blades that keep the bottom of the mash open, and so allows the sweet wort to drain away more easily.

Below: An African woman sits outside her home in Zambia brewing beer for her family.

Brewing

Brewing Up

Some of the names given to the utensils used in brewing still have a reassuring kitchen ring about them – a throwback to the days when brewing was a domestic chore. The brew-kettle for example – the vessel that the sweet wort is run into once it has been extracted from the malt – was once just that. Its other name, "the copper", is another relic from the past, because it would traditionally have been made of shining copper. Today in the large breweries the brew-kettles are usually closed and heated by internal steam coils. This is where the actual process of "brewing" takes place, as the liquid is boiled up with the hops for an hour or more. Some hops are added at the start of the boil to help clarify the wort and impart bitterness.

Late copper hops are sometimes added nearer the end, and boiled just long enough to release their oils, to provide the final aroma.

Turning Sugar to Alcohol

After the boiling is complete, the hopped wort passes through a filtering device known as a hopback, to remove the spent hops. It may also be passed through a whirlpool or centrifuge to remove unwanted proteins, before being cooled in preparation for fermentation.

Originally, the brew would have been cooled in large, open trays, but in modern breweries heat exchangers (paraflows) or chilling devices are usually used to speed up the process.

Fermenting

Once in the fermentation vessels, the yeast is pitched in. The millions of tiny fungus cells begin to feast on the sugar-rich wort for four to eight days, turning the sugars to alcohol and producing carbon-dioxide gas as part of their natural life cycle.

In top-fermenting ales the yeast rises to the surface, creating a heaving rocky head that

Left: A lauter tun is a filter vessel used in the decoction process when making bottom-fermented beers.

Above: In bottom-fermenting lagers, the yeast sinks to the base of the fermentation vessel.

Below: Huge, shiny coppers in the Saku Brewery, Estonia.

may need skimming to prevent it overflowing. In bottom-fermenting beers, the yeast eventually sinks to the bottom of the fermenting vessel.

Fermentation vessels range in size and shape from small, wooden rounds to vast stainless steel tanks. In the simplest and oldest systems large barrels are used for fermentation and the yeast bubbles up through the bung hole in the top. Modern breweries tend to prefer huge enclosed conical fermenters, stacked like upright rockets alongside the brewhouse.

When fermentation is complete, the yeast is then drained from the bottom of the fermentation vessels.

Maturing and Conditioning

After the initial, vigorous fermentation, the liquid, which is known as "green beer" is run into conditioning tanks where it is left to settle and mature.

The length, nature and location of this final process differs from beer to beer. For some ales, such as mild, this settling period is quite short. For bottom-fermenting beers the maturing process takes place at temperatures close to freezing and can last for many weeks, even months, purging and cleaning the brew and slowly completing the fermentation.

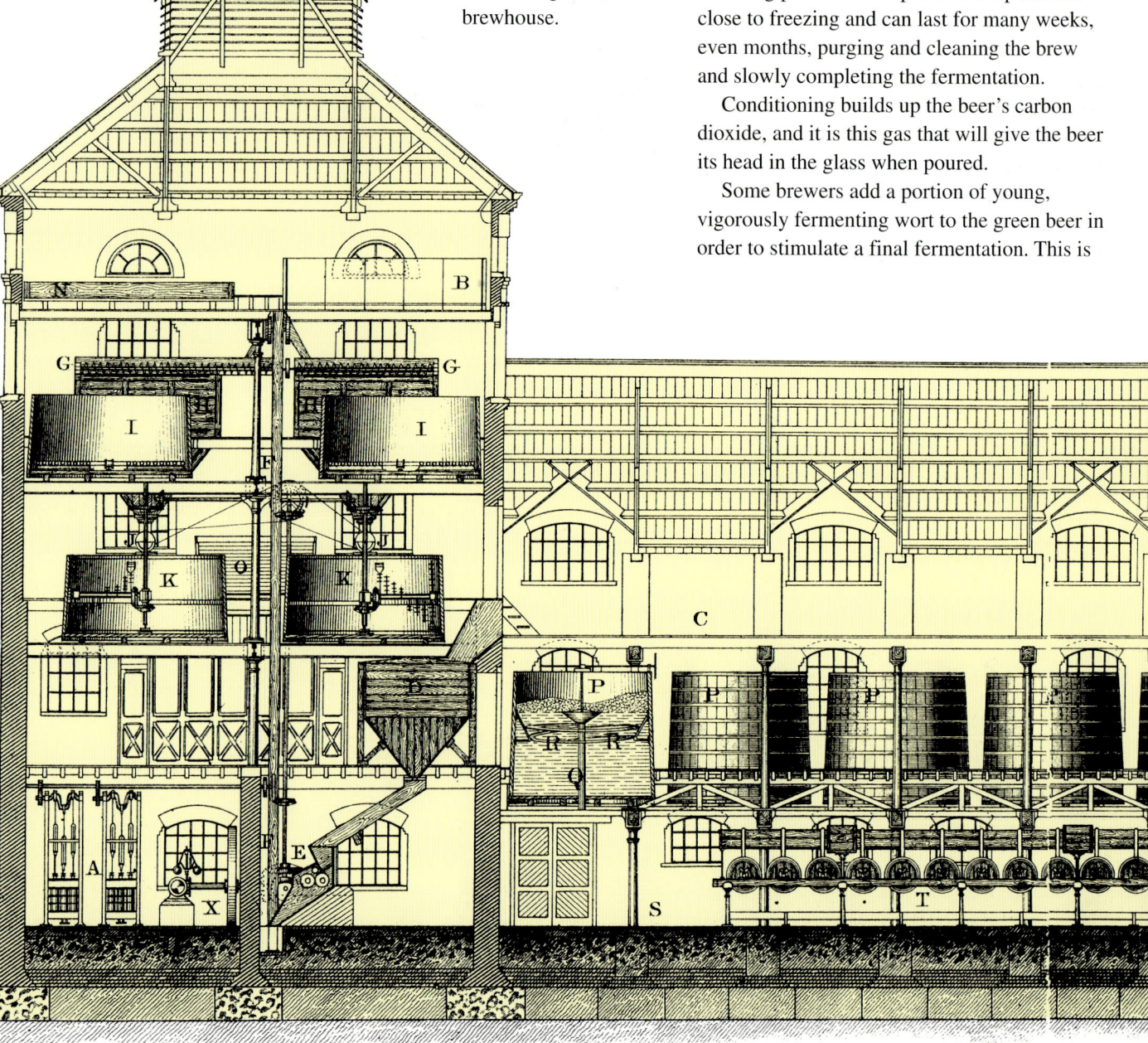

Conditioning builds up the beer's carbon dioxide, and it is this gas that will give the beer its head in the glass when poured.

Some brewers add a portion of young, vigorously fermenting wort to the green beer in order to stimulate a final fermentation. This is known as krausening. The modern, industrial alternative is to pump in extra carbon dioxide.

Most beers are filtered between conditioning and packaging at the brewery. Some breweries use a natural mineral known as kieselguhr on fine mesh screens; others use fine sheet filters.

Some traditional beers are racked directly into wooden or metal casks or bottles ready to go to the customer without filtration or any other processing. These beers are known as cask or bottle-conditioned brews.

Finings (a glutinous substance made from fish swim bladders) are also added to the cask to clear the beer.

The brew may also be primed with sugar in the bottle or cask, in order to encourage further fermentation. Dry hops may also be added in the cask to give the beer extra aroma. Some brewers even add extra yeast at this stage.

Cask-conditioned or bottle-conditioned brews continue to mature right until they are served, developing complex fruity flavours.

Left: Fermenting vats in Truman's brewery in the East End of London early in the 19th century.

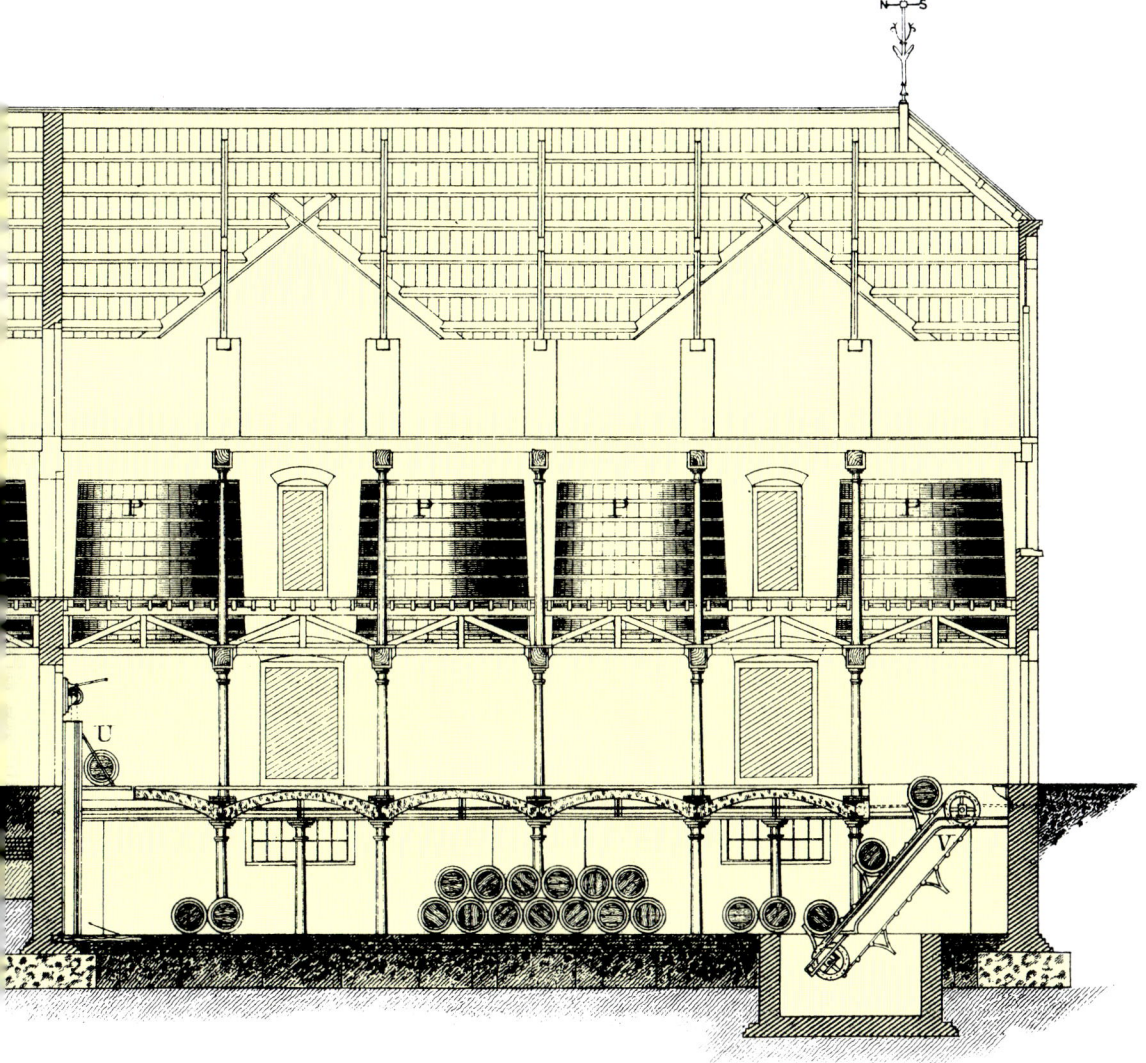

Left: A cross-section of a 19th-century brewery highlights the complex journey that the ingredients make during brewing. Modern breweries look quite different, but many of the items shown – mash tuns for example – can still be found.

A Pumps
B Cold liquor tank
C Malt store
D Malt hopper
E Malt rolls
F Elevator
G Malt screws
H Grist cases
I Hot liquor backs
J Mashing machines
K Mash tuns
N Cooler
O Refrigerator
P Fermenting tuns
Q Skimming apparatus
R Attemperator
S Tun room
T Cleaning casks
U Cask-lowering machine
V Cask-raising machine
X Steam engine

HI-TECH BREWING

Although the principles of brewing remain the same, there have been a number of attempted improvements in efficiency in the second half of the 20th century.

Above: Dominion Breweries of New Zealand pioneered the continuous brewing system.

Below: The brew is monitored at each stage to ensure a consistent end product.

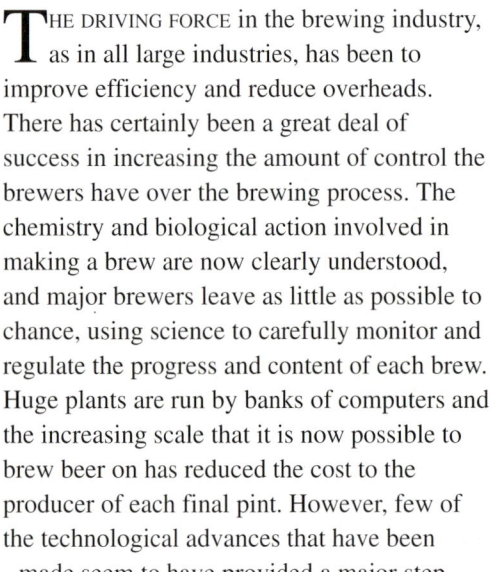

THE DRIVING FORCE in the brewing industry, as in all large industries, has been to improve efficiency and reduce overheads. There has certainly been a great deal of success in increasing the amount of control the brewers have over the brewing process. The chemistry and biological action involved in making a brew are now clearly understood, and major brewers leave as little as possible to chance, using science to carefully monitor and regulate the progress and content of each brew. Huge plants are run by banks of computers and the increasing scale that it is now possible to brew beer on has reduced the cost to the producer of each final pint. However, few of the technological advances that have been made seem to have provided a major step forward in beer quality.

INCREASING THE THROUGHPUT

Normally, brewing is done by the batch method. Individual brews are put through the process, from the raw ingredients to the finished product, one after another.

This system means that for some period, the equipment used at each stage is being unused while it waits for the next batch to arrive. It is also necessary to clean and prepare the vessels for the next batch.

Of course, in a large-scale operation this period of waiting time is minimized because the batches are sent quickly through one after another. However, some companies felt that they could make enormous cost savings if they could introduce continuous brewing, with wort and fermenting beer continually flowing through the plant.

This method was pioneered by Morton Coutts of Dominion Breweries of New Zealand in the 1950s, then Watney's developed a system in England in the 1970s. However, it did not provide the expected savings and the resulting flavour of the beer was disappointing.

Above: Computers now manage the complicated modern brewing process in many breweries.

High-gravity brewing

Another method of increasing the output of breweries that has been more widely adopted in the industry is high-gravity brewing. In this system the beer is first produced at higher strength than is intended for the finished product. The brew is then diluted at the end with water to bring it down to the required gravity – a technique rather like making orange squash.

High-gravity brewing allows the brewer to produce more beer than was previously possible in the same plant.

Some companies are now investigating taking this concept even further and brewing just one high-gravity bland brew that can then be diluted to produce different strength beers and, through the addition of different flavourings, colourings and extracts, used to produce a range of different products.

BIO-SCIENCE AT WORK

Advances in bio-technology and genetics mean that it is now possible to manipulate and control the process of fermentation by changing the nature of the yeast. Enzymes have even been used by some brewers, notably in America, to speed up the brewing process.

Biological science has also been employed

in the brewer's fight against contamination, in the form of techniques for disinfecting and cleaning the equipment in the brewery.

Pasteurization
It is now common practice for manufacturers to attempt to prolong the shelf-life and stability of their products through pasteurization. Virtually all canned and many bottled beers are pasteurized, as are pressurized keg beers for serving at the bar.

During pasteurization the beer is heated in order to kill off any rogue bacteria that may have entered it during the brewing process, and that may turn it sour. One method of pasteurizing is to spray the bottles or cans with hot water for about an hour; another method is to spray extremely hot water or steam over the can or bottle for a minute or so.

Pasteurization not only eradicates any unwanted organisms in the beer, but it also completely kills the yeast in the beer and inevitably the flavour and character of the beer are affected. Pasteurized beers are usually artificially carbonated in order to give them a semblance of life when served and to ensure a satisfactory head on the glass.

Indeed, Louis Pasteur, who developed the process for wine, not beer, noted in a footnote to the English edition of *Etudes sur la Bière*, "This process is less successful in the case of beer than in that of wine, for the delicacy of flavour which distinguishes beer is affected by the heat."

Some leading lager brewers, such as Grolsch, have demonstrated that it is possible even for widely distributed beers to remain unpasteurized.

Above: The modern Sapporo brewery in Hokkaido, Japan, where beer brewing is a science.

Below: Huge lager tanks outside a German brewery highlight the sheer scale of today's breweries.

FROM BREWERY TO GLASS

The advent of metal casks and cans has led to a revolution in the way that beer is packaged and sold. Consistency and reliability have improved, but often at the expense of quality and character.

Above: Once the beer is brewed the next problem for the brewer is getting it into the glass.

Below: A cooper and his apprentice hard at work in their brewery workshop.

UNTIL WELL INTO THE 20TH CENTURY, most beer was served at the bar or tavern directly from wooden casks. The casks rested on a stillage (a wooden framework) in order to allow them to be tilted as they were emptied. If the casks were kept in a cellar, a pump would be used to raise the beer to the bar at the point of sale. The wooden casks that held the beer were usually made and maintained by each brewery in its own cooperage. Huge pyramids of wooden casks were one of the wonders of brewery yards.

CASK'S PROGRESS

Coopering – the art of building and repairing the wooden casks – was vital. It played a major part in the brewing business because without the casks the beer in the brewhouse would never reach the thirsty customers waiting at the bars. The casks had to be soundly constructed. They had to be able to withstand the heavy handling involved in

Above: Even today some brewers maintain the tradition of beer from the wood, keeping the coopers' ancient craft alive.

transporting them about the countryside. They also had to resist the pressure of the live beer inside without leaking. The most suitable wood for this purpose was the strong, but flexible, Memel oak from the Baltic, which was exported around the world.

Coopering was a highly skilled craft and the apprentices underwent as much as five years training. Some large breweries boasted extensive cooperages employing hundreds of coopers. In the 1880s Bass, in Burton-on-Trent, England, had a stave store for storing loose wood that covered 25 acres.

A revolution

In the 1930s an innovation almost wiped out the coopers' trade: metal casks made from stainless steel or aluminium were introduced. These containers were lighter, cheaper and required less maintenance than wood. Within 40 years the metal newcomers had largely replaced handsome, handmade wooden casks.

Above: Large, high-speed bottling and canning plants were made possible as technology improved.

Above: The old and the new, as a dray team gets loaded up with modern metal kegs.

However, some breweries have hung on to the traditional oak barrels, partly because of the flavour and colour that the wood adds to the beer as it sits inside, and partly because during hot weather a wooden cask offers the beer better insulation from ruinous high temperatures.

BOTTLING UP

The brewing industry has long sought to provide more convenient containers to enable its customers to carry their beer home in small quantities. Bottled beer is much older than many imagine.

Earthenware vessels date back many centuries, and hand-manufactured glass bottles, which first appeared in the 17th century, were especially favoured for exporting beers.

Bottled beer came into more widespread use once steam-powered glass-bottle-making machines were introduced in the mid-19th century. Mechanization allowed bottles to be produced and filled with drink much more quickly and cheaply than before, and enabled the brewers to develop their own mass-produced, distinctively shaped bottles.

The sealing problem

Most early beer bottles were coloured brown or green in order to prevent the light penetrating and spoiling the contents.

The bottles were originally corked like wine bottles, but then Englishman Henry Barrett patented the internal screw stopper in 1872, which enabled the bottle to be re-sealed.

The metal crown cap, which was patented by an American, William Painter, followed the screw stopper 20 years later. It may not offer the advantage of being able to reseal the bottle, but it is cheap and lends itself to mass-production techniques. It is still the most common method used for sealing bottles.

Moving back to tradition

The bottled beer trade really took off after 1900. The emphasis was on bright, sparkling beer that looked good through the glass. The content of the bottles was increasingly chilled, filtered, carbonated and pasteurized.

In recent years, more flavoursome bottle-conditioned beers with a sediment, which continue to mature after they have been packaged, have made a comeback. In Belgium many bottled beers, such as the famous Trappist ale Orval, continue to mature in the bottle and contain a heavy sediment. In France, bière de garde is traditionally bottle-conditioned and improves with age like a good wine. It is often produced in wine-shaped bottles and sealed with a wine cork.

Below: Bottles of French bière de garde from farmhouses in northern France are traditionally corked.

DAWN OF THE SIX-PACK

The tin can – perhaps the ultimate convenience package for beer – appeared in the 1930s. Solid foods and soups had been sold in cans since early in the 19th century, but tinned beer presented greater difficulties. A beer-filled can would have to withstand extremely high pressures from within or it would burst along the seam. Another problem was that the tin tainted the taste of whatever was kept inside. In addition, tin cans at that time were more expensive than glass bottles. Breweries simply were not interested.

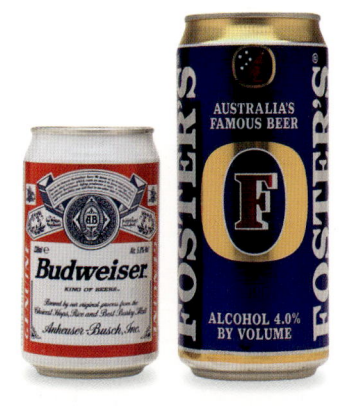

Above: Despite initial reluctance, brewers the world over have now adopted cans as a convenient packaging medium.

Above: An early can of Coronation Brew with a coned top.

Breaking into the market

After the end of Prohibition in the United States, beer sales shot up and American can manufacturers were eager to break into the glass-dominated beer market. One firm, CanCo, eventually managed to develop a tin can with an internal lining, capable of resisting the pressures placed upon it by beer. In 1933 the pioneering company persuaded a hard-pressed brewery, Kreuger of Newark, New Jersey, to test out the tinny brew. The trial was a success and in January 1935 the company launched two canned beer brands – Kreuger's Finest Beer and Cream Ale.

A good response

The shiny novelty went down well with the public. The compact cans were lighter to carry home than a bottle, and fitted more easily into the refrigerators that were now appearing in every kitchen. Other companies were quick to seize on the new marketing opportunity and by the end of the year, 37 breweries, including the giants Pabst and Schlitz, were rattling out tinned supplies. The six-pack era had arrived in America.

Gradually the trend for canned beer spread and as cans were being churned off the production lines in the US, the first Europeans took their tentative steps forwards in the packaging revolution. The first brewery to can

Right: Beer's image improved so much after the end of Prohibition that by the 1950s the new refrigerators appearing in most American homes were stocked with cans of beer alongside other everyday groceries.

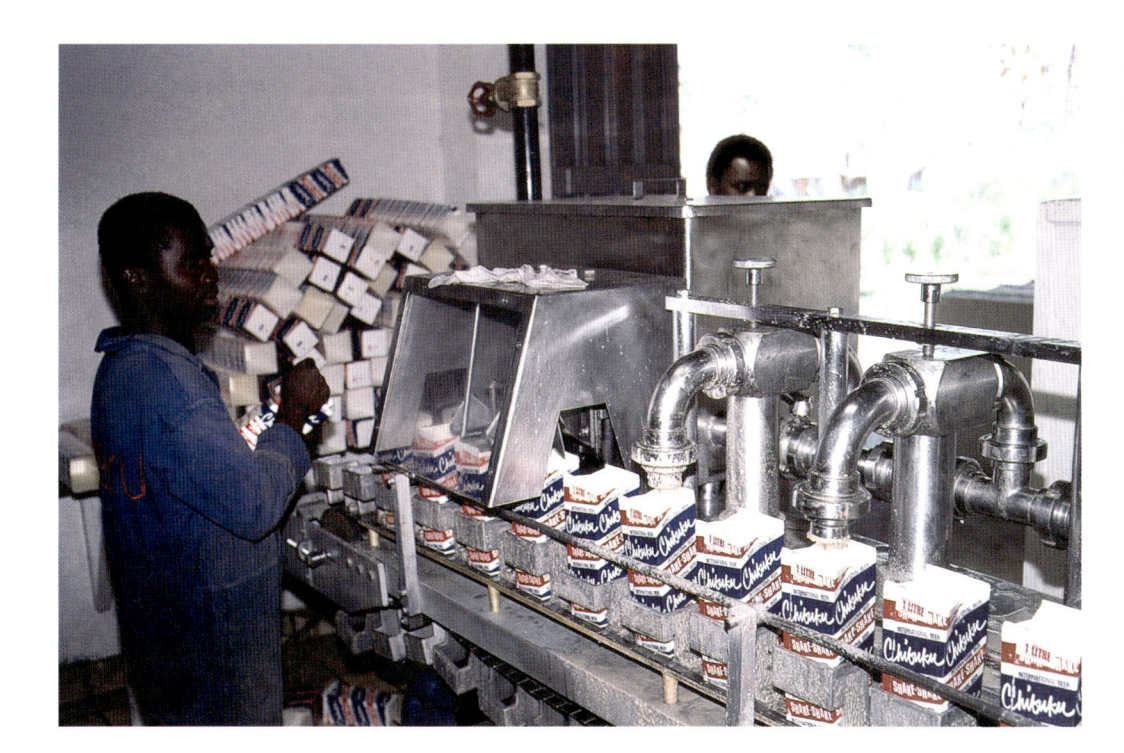

Left: Perhaps the ultimate in convenience packaging is the cardboard carton, seen in use here in Malawi.

beer in Europe was the Felinfoel Brewery of Llanelli in Wales. In a bid to boost the declining local tinplate industry of South Wales, it launched its pale ale in a can in December 1935.

Reluctant market

The brewing industry was pressed into the move to canned beers to some extent by the can manufacturers. The brewers' initial reluctance to make this innovation was understandable. The can has never really proved an ideal container for quality beer. At best, it provides a convenient, throwaway package, but the flavour and aroma of the processed contents often leave much to be desired. But as cheaper aluminium cans were introduced, the economic argument for canning beer was hard to resist.

Perhaps it is significant that relatively few wines have appeared in cans, and that in some major beer-drinking countries like the Czech Republic and Germany, the consumers have been reluctant to accept their favourite beers in what they see as an inferior container.

In Britain, where beer consumers have a long tradition of drinking draught beer, the breweries have ploughed a lot of money and effort into trying to make their take-home products as similar as possible in taste and "feel" to their cousins served in the pub. In the early 1990s beer manufacturers trumpeted a breakthrough in this area with the introduction of the "widget" in the can.

This small plastic device sits in the bottom of a can and when the ring pull is removed, the release of pressure triggers an injection of nitrogen into the beer, to provide it with a creamy, thick head. Although the feel of the beer is certainly improved, it is doubtful that this ingenious device has actually improved the taste of the beer.

Below: Cans are cleaned, filled and sealed on a prodigious scale and with hair-raising speed on modern canning production lines.

STYLES OF BEER

The title "beer" runs the gamut from dark, hearty ales to tangy, spritzy gueuzes. The myriad different tastes, colours, flavours and aromas can, to some extent, be squeezed into groupings with similar characteristics and methods of production.

NEWSPAPERS AND MAGAZINES have had tasteful columns about the mysteries of wine for many years, but it is only recently that writers have begun to discuss beer in the same way. Beer is much more complex than wine. Wine is based on a single ingredient – grapes. Beer is a fine balance between two – malt and hops. The variety of hops is as great as the variety of grapes and there are many different styles of malt and different cereals. In addition, there is an exotic store of extra spices for the more adventurous brewer. Today, interest in local styles and different qualities has never been greater. Drinkers increasingly appreciate that there is a rich variety of beer tastes to explore around the world.

Above: The names of abbey beers may be misleading since most are now brewed under licence by commercial breweries.

Below: Ale is a convenient, catch-all term that is generally used to mean beer made using top-fermenting yeast.

ABBEY BEERS

Strong fruity ales, abbey beers are brewed in Belgium by commercial companies, sometimes under licence from religious communities. They copy the style of the surviving beers produced in monasteries, or name their brews after a church or saint. Examples include Leffe from Interbrew, Grimbergen from the Union Brewery and Maredsous from Moortgat. (See Trappist.)

ALE

Nowadays this is a vague term meaning any top-fermented beer. It is one of the two main branches of the beer family, the other being lager. Of the two, ale is the older, dating back thousands of years. England is the country where ales are now most commonly brewed.

ALT

Alt is the German word meaning "traditional" or "old", and in the context of Altbier it indicates a bitter-tasting brew produced by the ancient style of brewing using top-fermentation. Alt is a copper-coloured aromatic ale, made in the city of Düsseldorf and a few other cities in northern Germany. It is a firm-bodied but quite bitter beer that contains just over 4.5% alcohol. Major, well-known brands include Diebels, Schlosser and Uerige.

Barley Wine
Barley wine is the English name for a powerful, almost syrupy, strong ale, that is usually sold in small nip-size bottles. These well-matured brews can be golden or dark in colour. The darker versions of barley wine were once called Stingo.

Berliner Weisse
A light, sharply acidic German wheat beer made predominantly in Berlin, this refreshing brew is relatively low in alcohol and is often laced with a dash of green woodruff or raspberry juice to add colour to its cloudy white (weisse) appearance.

Bière de Garde
A top-fermenting "beer for keeping" from north-west France, this was originally made in farmhouses, but is now produced by commercial breweries. This style produces medium to strong, spicy ales; some are bottle-conditioned, and many are sealed with champagne-style wired corks.

Bitter
The distinctive style of draught ale in England and Wales is generally served in pubs. It is usually dry and hoppy with an alcohol content of 3–5%. Traditionally reddish amber in colour, paler varieties are now proving popular in England. Stronger versions used to be called Best or Special.

Black Beer
In Germany, Schwarzbier is a strong-tasting, bitter-chocolate lager. It is not a stout but a very dark lager and is a speciality of eastern Germany, particularly around Bernau. The town of Kostritz in the former East Germany is noted for its black lager, and Kulmbach and Erlangen are also known for their deep brown beers. This style is also made in Japan.

In England, especially Yorkshire, black beers are strong, pitch-black, treacly malt extracts, usually bottled for mixing with lemonade to make distinctive shandies.

Bock
A strong malty, warming German beer of about 6.5% alcohol, bock was originally brewed for the colder months. Traditionally dark in colour, today it is more likely to be golden-bronze. This powerful smooth brew originated in Einbeck in Lower Saxony, but is now more associated with Bavaria. Bock is also produced in Austria, the Netherlands and other countries surrounding Germany. The word bock means "billy goat", and a goat's head often features on the label. The brew is sometimes linked with seasonal festivals, such as Maibock which celebrates the arrival of spring. Extra-potent versions are called doppelbocks (and are chiefly associated with Bavaria), with more than 7% alcohol, such as Paulaner Salvator. Eisbocks, in which frozen water is removed from the beer, are even more powerful. This brew (10%) is the speciality of Reichelbrau of Kulmbach.

Brown Ale
A sweetish, bottled mild ale, dark in colour and low in alcohol, from England, brown ale was once a popular workers' drink, although sales have declined heavily in recent years. The north-east of the country produces stronger,

Above: Bitter is not bitter in taste as its name might suggest. It usually has a floral, fruity flavour.

Above: Bocks were originally drunk by fasting monks because they were considered nutritious.

STYLES OF BEER

Above: Brown ale was one of the traditional drinks of the working classes in England. Nowadays sales have declined.

drier versions like the well-known Newcastle Brown Ale.

Belgium boasts its own sweet-and-sour brown ales from East Flanders. The main producer is Liefmans of Oudenaarde. The sour taste comes from a slow simmering rather than a boil, and from the addition of a lactic yeast. Other producers include Cnudde, also of Oudenaarde, the nearby Roman Brewery and Vanden Stock.

CHILLI BEER
Produced by only a handful of American breweries this is an odd, slow-burning speciality. The Pike Place Brewery of Seattle produces an occasional Cerveza Rosanna Red Chilli Ale, while the hotter Crazy Ed's Cave Creek Chilli Beer of Phoenix, Arizona, has a whole chilli pod in each bottle. It reputedly goes well with Mexican food.

CREAM ALE
A sweetish, smooth, golden ale from the United States, cream ale was originally introduced by ale brewers trying to copy the Pilsner style. Some cream ales are made by blending ales with bottom-fermenting beers.

DIÄT PILS
Nothing to do with dieting, diät pils is lager which undergoes a thorough fermentation which removes nearly all the sugars from the bottom-fermented, Pilsner-derived brew. This leaves a strong, dry-tasting beer, which is still packed with calories in the alcohol. It was originally brewed as a beer suitable for diabetics, rather than slimmers. Because it misled many, the word "diät" has now been removed.

DOPPELBOCK
An extra-strong bock beer; doppelbock is not double in strength, but usually around 7.5% alcohol. It is rich and warming. The names of the leading Bavarian brands usually end in "ator", Salvator from Paulaner of Munich, for example.

DORTMUNDER
Dortmunder is a strong, full-bodied export style of lager from Dortmund in Germany, the biggest brewing city in Europe. It was originally brewed for export and was once sold under this name across the globe, but is now declining in popularity. Malty, dry and full-bodied, these brews usually have an alcohol strength of around 5.5%, being firmer and less aromatic than a Pilsner. The leading examples include DAB, Kronen and DUB.

DRY BEER
First produced in Japan by the Asahi Brewery in 1987, this is a super diät pils with a parching effect, which was widely adopted in North America. The beer taste is so clean it has been swept away almost entirely through further fermentation.

Dry beer, in which more of the sugars are turned to alcohol leaving little taste, was developed in Japan and launched in America in 1988. After an initial surge in sales when Anheuser-Busch introduced Bud Dry, the market has faded almost completely away.

DUNKEL
German lagers were traditionally dark, and these soft, malty brown beers are associated with Munich, often being known as Münchner. Like the paler hell, they contain around 4.5% alcohol. Most of the major Munich breweries produce a dunkel.

Duppel/Double
This is a term used to describe dark, medium-strength Trappist and abbey beers in Belgium.

Eisbock
An extra-potent bock, eisbock is produced by freezing the brew and removing some of the frozen water to leave behind more concentrated alcohol. The most notable producer is Kulmbacher Reichelbrau in Northern Bavaria. Eisbock is the original ice beer.

Export
This term was originally used to denote a better-quality beer, worth selling abroad. The Dortmunder style is also known as Dortmunder Export, since it became popular around the world. In Scotland, the term export is widely adopted for premium ales.

Faro
Once the most common manifestation of Belgian lambic beer, faro is a weak lambic sweetened with sugar. Now this style has largely disappeared.

Framboise/Frambozen
These are Flemish and French names for a Belgium fruit beer made by adding raspberries to a lambic. Framboise has a sparkling, pink champagne character and the raspberries impart a light, fruity flavour. Because the whole fruit is too soft, producers usually add raspberry syrup. In recent years a whole variety of other fruit juices have been tried, from peaches to bananas, with varying degrees of success.

Ginger Beer
Despite its name, this is a refreshing, low or no-alcohol soft drink flavoured with root ginger. However, long before the hop appeared, ginger was used in beer and some pioneering micro-brewers are trying it again: Salopian in England adds ginger to its dark wheat beer, Gingersnap.

Green Beer
Any young beer which has not had time to mature is known as a green beer. The term is also used to denote a beer made with organic malt and hops. Organic green beer is known as biologique in France (where Castelain makes an organic beer called Jade) and biologisch in Germany. In Scotland, the Caledonian Brewery of Edinburgh has pioneered organic ale with Golden Promise.

Gueuze
This is a ripe blend of old and new Belgian lambics. By blending young and old lambics, a secondary fermentation is triggered. The resulting distinctive, sparkling beer, often sold in corked bottles like champagne to withstand the pressure, packs a fruity, sour, dry taste. Blending is such an art that some producers do not brew, but buy in their wort. Often this beer is matured for many more months in the bottle. In some cases the secondary fermentation is triggered by the addition of various fruits. Traditionally gueuze should not be filtered, pasteurized or sweetened, though some more commercial brands do all three.

Heavy
Scottish brewers use this term to describe a standard strength ale, between a Light and an Export. A "wee heavy" is a bottled strong ale, the wee referring to the small nip-size of the bottle.

Hefe
The German word for yeast is used to describe a beer that is unfiltered, with a sediment in the bottle. Draught beers "mit Hefe" are usually cloudy.

Hell
This word means pale or light in German and indicates a mild, malty golden lager, often from Munich. Notable examples include Hacker-Pschorr and Augustiner.

Honey Beer
The Celts and other ancient peoples used to make mead from fermented honey. They also produced a beer,

Above: Several breweries have sprung up producing "green" beer using only organic ingredients.

Below: The word "Hefe" on a label indicates that the beer still contains yeast.

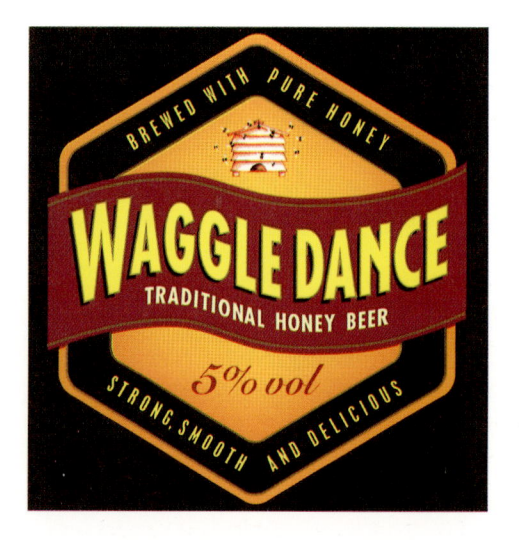

Styles of Beer

Right: The attractively named Waggle Dance honey beer brewed by Ward's of Sheffield is a revival of an old traditional drink of the Celtic people.

Far right: A selection of IPAs.

Below: US brewers have followed the Canadian innovation of ice beers.

bragot, to which honey was often added as a soft sweetener. A hazy honey brew called Golden Mead Ale was produced in England by Hope & Anchor Breweries of Sheffield, and was widely exported until the early 1960s. Today, a few breweries have revived the style, notably Ward's of Sheffield with Waggle Dance and Enville Ales of Staffordshire. Some new American brewers also use honey, as do the innovative Belgian De Dolle Brouwers in their Boskeun beer.

Ice Beer

A chilling innovation of the early 1990s; the brew is frozen during maturation to produce a purified beer, with the ice crystals removed to increase the strength.

Many ice beers were originally developed in Canada by Labatt and contain around 5.5% alcohol. Canadian brewers Labatt and Molson introduced the new beer style in 1993 in which the beer is frozen after fermentation, giving a cleaner, almost smoothed away flavour. Sometimes the ice crystals are removed, concentrating the beer. Most major US brewers have launched their own brands such as Bud Ice and Miller's Icehouse, but ice beer still accounts for less than 4% of the beer market.

In 1996, Tennent's of Scotland produced a Super Ice with a strength of 8.6%.

Imperial Stout
See Stout.

IPA

The words behind the initials betray IPAs imperial origins – India Pale Ale. This strong, heavily hopped beer was brewed in Britain, notably in Burton-on-Trent by companies like Allsopp and Bass. The recipe was designed to withstand the long sea voyages to distant parts of the British Empire like India. According to legend, a cargo of 300 casks of Bass's East India Pale Ale was wrecked off the port of Liverpool in 1827. Some of the rescued beer was sold locally and won instant fame among English drinkers. Specialist American brewers like Bert Grant's Yakima Brewing Company now probably produce the most authentic versions.

Irish Ale

A soft, slightly sweet reddish ale from the "Emerald Isle". Top and bottom-fermenting versions are brewed commercially. This ale followed many of the Irish in migrating to other lands. George Killian Letts, a member of the Letts family who brewed Ruby Ale in County Wexford until 1956, licensed the French brewery Pelforth to produce George Killian's Bière Rousse and the American brewers Coors to produce Killian's Irish Red. Smithwick's of Kilkenny (owned by Guinness) is the best-known ale in Ireland today.

Kölsch

The refreshing golden beer of Cologne may look like a Pilsner (though it may sometimes be cloudy), but its light, subtle fruity taste reveals it to be a top-fermenting ale. Its fleeting aromatic nature masks an alcohol content of 4–5%.

Kölsch is produced only by some 20 breweries in and around the busy cathedral city of Cologne and it is usually served in small glasses. The leading producers include Kuppers and Fruh.

KRIEK

In this Belgian lambic beer, secondary fermentation is stimulated by adding cherries to give a dry, fruity flavour and deep colour. This is not a novelty drink, but draws on a long tradition of using local fruit to flavour an already complex brew, balancing the lambic sourness and providing an almond character from the cherry stones. The kriek is a small dark cherry grown near Brussels.

KRISTALL

This term, taken from the German word for a crystal-clear beer, usually indicates a filtered wheat beer or Weizenbier.

LAGER

Lager is one of the two main branches of the beer family. The word lager is derived from the German word "to store". In Britain it refers to any golden, bottom-fermented beer, but elsewhere it has little meaning, apart from a general word for beer.

LAMBIC

The wild beers of Belgium have their roots deep in history. One of the most primitive beers brewed on earth, these spontaneously fermenting beers are unique to Belgium, or to be more exact, to an area to the west of Brussels in the Senne Valley.

Lambic brewers use at least 30% unmalted wheat in order to produce a milky wort from the mash. Old hops are used, as they are only required for their preservative value, not for their flavour or aroma.

Unlike most other beer styles, in which a carefully cultivated yeast is used to ferment the wort, the wheat brew used to produce lambic beer is left exposed to the air to allow spontaneous fermentation to happen from wild yeasts in the atmosphere. As in previous centuries, this beer is only brewed in the cooler months of the year, as the wild yeasts would be too unpredictable in summer. The fermenting wort is then run into large wooden casks and left to age in dark, dusty galleries from three months to many years.

The result is a unique, tart, sour beer, probably similar to the ales made in ancient times. The taste is almost like a flat, acidic cider, which attacks the tongue and sucks in the cheeks. It has an alcohol content of around 5%. This can be drunk young on its own, often on draught in cafés in the Brussels area, but it is usually blended with older lambics to produce gueuze. Sometimes fruit is added to create framboise (raspberry) or kriek (cherry) beers. The lambic range of beers is mainly produced by small, speciality brewers, like Boon, Cantillon, De Troch, Girardin and Timmermans. But there are a few more commercial brands, notably Belle-Vue (part of Interbrew) and St Louis.

LIGHT ALE

In England, this term indicates a bottled low-gravity bitter. In Scotland, it means the weakest brew, a beer light in strength although it may well be dark in colour.

Far left: Apart from in Britain, the term lager is used generally for beer.

Below: The term lambic indicates a Belgian wheat beer that is spontaneously fermented by wild, airborne yeast.

Styles of Beer

Lite
In North America, this term is used to describe a thin, low-calorie beer, the best-known being Miller Lite. In some countries, Australia for instance, lite can mean low in alcohol.

Low Alcohol
Since the late 1980s, many breweries throughout the world have added low- or no-alcohol brews to their beer range, usually in response to increasingly strict drink-driving laws. Low alcohol (or LA) can contain as much as 2.5% alcohol. Alcohol-free brews should contain no more than 0.05%. Some of these near beers are produced using yeasts which create little alcohol, or the fermentation is cut short.

In others the alcohol is removed from a normal beer by distillation or reverse osmosis. It has proved difficult to provide an acceptable beer taste. Some of the more successful brews, Clausthaler from Frankfurt in Germany and Birell from Hürlimann of Zurich in Switzerland, now sell or licence their low- or no-alcohol beers across many countries.

Malt Liquor
In the United States, this term indicates a strong lager, often made with a high amount of sugar to produce a thin but potent brew. These beers are designed to deliver a strong alcoholic punch (around 6–8%) but little else. They are light beers with a kick, often cheaply made with a high proportion of sugar and using enzymes to create more alcohol. Sales of malt liquor account for about 4% of the total American beer market.

Märzen
A full-bodied copper-coloured lager, this beer style originated in Vienna, but developed in Munich as a stronger Märzen (March) brew (6% alcohol), which was laid down in March, to allow it to mature over the summer for drinking at the Oktoberfest after the harvest. It has largely been replaced in Germany by more golden "Festbiere". Smooth and malty, most are now stronger versions of the golden hell, containing more than 5.5% alcohol. Notable examples include Spaten Ur-Märzen and Hofbrauhaus Oktoberfest.

Mild
Mild was the dominant ale in England and Wales until the 1960s, and later in some regions. It is a relatively low-gravity malty beer, usually lightly hopped, and can be dark or pale in colour. Mild was traditionally the workers' drink and would be sold on draught in the pub or club. Today, the style has vanished from many areas; it survives mainly in the industrial West Midlands and the north-west of England.

Milk Stout
See Stout.

Münchner
The German name for a beer from Munich traditionally refers to the city's brown, malty lager style.

Oatmeal Stout
See Stout.

Old Ale
This strong, well-matured, rich, dark ale is usually sold as a seasonal beer in England as a winter warmer. Sometimes such ales are used as stock beers for blending with fresher brews.

Oud Bruin
Old Browns in the Netherlands are weak, sweetish lagers.

Oyster Stout
See Stout.

Pale Ale
An English bottled beer, pale ale is stronger than light ale and is usually based on the brewery's best bitter. See IPA.

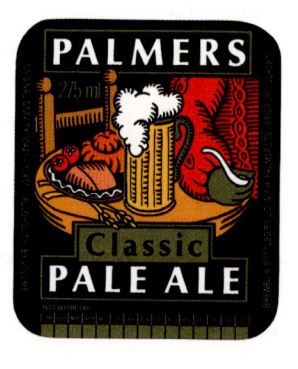

Above: In Miller Lite more of the sugar is turned to alcohol in the brewing process to produce a lower-calorie beer.

Below: Relatively low alcohol, mild is usually a dark brown ale which was originally brewed for English workers.

Pilsner

Strictly speaking, Pilsner is a golden, hoppy, aromatic lager from the Bohemian Czech town of Plzen (Pilsen in German), where this classic style was first produced in 1842. The original Pilsner Urquell (original source) is still brewed there. Czech Pilsner has a complex character with a flowery hop aroma and a dry finish.

This golden classic has spawned a thousand imitators, some excellent, others pale, lacklustre imitations of the original. Variations on the style now dominate the world beer market.

Pilsner is now the predominant lager beer of Germany. German Pilsners are dry and hoppy with a light, golden colour. They contain around 5% alcohol and often lack the smooth maltiness of the original Czech version.

Leading German brands include Warsteiner, Bitburger and Herforder.

Left: The original Pilsner comes from Plzen in the Czech Republic, but it has spawned many imitators.

Porter

The origins of porter are shrouded in myths and legends. It was said to have been invented in London in 1722 by Ralph Harwood when he grew tired of making Three Threads, a popular drink of the day, by mixing strong, brown and old ales. He decided to brew one beer – or entire butt – combining the characteristics of all three.

In fact, porter was the product of the world's first major breweries, which were rising in London at this time. By brewing on a large scale with huge vessels, they were able to concoct a beer that was much more stable with far better keeping qualities than previous ales – porter.

The first porter was a traditional London brown mild ale which was much more heavily hopped than usual in order to improve its keeping qualities. The beer was then matured for months in vast vats, to increase its alcoholic strength. Older brews were then blended with fresher ones to produce an "entire" beer.

Only major brewers, such as Barclay, Truman and Whitbread, could afford to build the expensive plants that were necessary to produce beer on this scale and to tie up so much capital in maturing beer. In return for their investment, they captured the English capital's beer market, as porter was much more reliable than previous ales. The economies of scale in its production also made it cheaper. Porter proved so successful that it was widely distributed and exported.

Enterprising brewers elsewhere, like Guinness in Dublin, followed this example and began to brew their own porter. Sales gradually declined in the 19th century as it was replaced in popularity by paler ales and only the stronger or "stouter" porters survived. The name is still used around the world today to indicate a brown beer.

In the Baltic countries, strong porters are still made, based on the original export brews. Some new micro-brewers have also tried to revive the dark, dry style in England and North America.

Porter, however, was never a craft beer. It flowed from the Industrial Revolution. It was the first mass-produced beer.

Below: Dark porters have diminished in popularity relative to when they were first introduced.

Rauchbier

The intense smoky flavour of these German smoked beers from the region of Franconia comes from malt that has been dried over moist beechwood fires. There are nine breweries in the town of Bamburg that produce this dark, bottom-fermented speciality. Leading examples include Schlenkerla and Spezial.

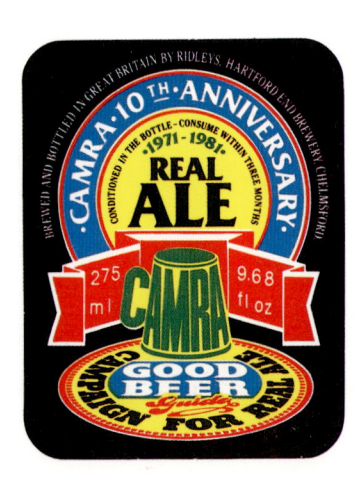

Above: The Campaign for Real Ale celebrated its tenth anniversary with a traditional brewed beer.

REAL ALE
The British drinkers' consumer organization, CAMRA, the Campaign for Real Ale, devised this name for traditional cask-conditioned beer which continues to mature in the pub cellar. Real ale is not filtered or pasteurized.

RED BEER
The reddish sour beers of West Flanders in Belgium are sometimes dubbed the Burgundies of Belgium. The colour comes from using Vienna malt. The prime producer is Rodenbach of Roeselare, who matures its beers in a remarkable forest of huge oak vats.

Younger brews are blended with old to create the distinctive Rodenbach brand. Some of the more mature beer is bottled on its own as the classic Grand Cru. Other brands include Petrus from Bavik and Duchesse de Bourgogne from Verhaeghe of Vichte.

ROGGEN
Only a few breweries make this German or Austrian rye beer. Some English and American breweries have started to use rye to add flavour to barley malt, and one American brewer produces its own Roggen Rye.

ROOT BEER
An American temperance soft drink, not a beer, it was originally flavoured with sassafras root bark. Root beer is boiled but not fermented.

RUSSIAN STOUT
See Stout.

SAISON/SEZUEN
This Belgian speciality beer is now hard to find. A refreshing, slightly sour summer style, saison (which means "season" in French) is mainly made in rural breweries in the French-speaking Wallonia region, some of which have closed in recent years.

The orange, highly hopped, top-fermenting ales are brewed in winter and then laid down to condition in sturdy wine bottles for drinking in the hot summer months. They are sold in corked bottles after ageing. Some also contain added spices like ginger.

Small producers include Silly, Dupont and Vapeur. The larger Du Bocq brewery makes Saison Régal, while in Flanders Martens of Bocholt produces Sezuens.

Above: The De Dolle brewery in Silly, Belgium, produces a strong, dark, Scotch-style ale.

SCHWARZBIER
See Black Beer.

SCOTCH ALE
Scotland's ales, brewed many miles from the nearest hop field, tend to be more malty in character than English beers. Bitters are called Light, Heavy, Special or Export in Scotland, depending on their strength, or are sometimes rated 60/-, 70/- or 80/- shillings according to an old pricing system.

Bottled Scotch Ale in Belgium is the name given to a powerful, rich ale, which is often brewed in Belgium itself.

STEAM BEER
An American cross between a bottom-fermented beer and an ale, steam beer was originally made in the Gold Rush days in California. It was brewed with lager yeasts at warm ale temperatures, using wide, shallow pans. Casks of this lively brew were said to hiss like steam when tapped. Now it is brewed only by the Anchor Steam Brewery of San Francisco.

STEINBIER
German "stone beer" is brewed using a primitive method of heating, in which red-hot rocks are lowered into the brew to bring it to the boil. The sizzling stones become covered in burnt sugars and are then added back to the beer at the maturation stage to spark a second fermentation. This smoky, full-bodied brew is made only by Rauchenfels at Altenmünster near Augsburg.

Stout

One of the classic styles of ale, originally a stout porter, stout has survived and prospered thanks to its sharp contrast in taste and colour to the popular Pilsner – and also to the determined marketing and enterprise of one brewer, Guinness of Ireland.

This dry black brew is made with a proportion of dark roasted barley in the mash and is heavily hopped to give its distinctive taste. Draught stout tends to be much creamier and smoother than the more distinctive bottled beer, because it uses nitrogen gas in its dispenser. Guinness also produce a much heavier Foreign Extra Stout for export. Some other countries also produce dry stout, notably Australia, with fine examples from Cooper's of Adelaide and Tooth's of Sydney.

Besides dry or bitter stout, there are a number of variations of this dark style:

Milk or Sweet Stout

This is a much weaker and smoother bottled English stout, originally called Milk Stout because of the use of lactose (milk sugar). The name was banned in Britain in 1946 because of the implication that milk is added to the brew, though it is still used in some countries such as South Africa and Malta. The leading brand, Whitbread's Mackeson, still maintains a creamy connection through the sketch of a milk churn on the label. The Boston Beer Company in America produces a Samuel Adams Cream Stout. In addition, there are stronger tropical sweet stouts, notably Dragon brewed in Jamaica and Lion which comes from Sri Lanka.

Oatmeal Stout

Many sweet stouts were sold as nourishing, restorative drinks for invalids. Some were further strengthened by the addition of oats. Once a popular bottled brew, most oatmeal stouts have vanished, but a few have been revived, including Sam Smith's Oatmeal Stout from Yorkshire in England and Maclay's Oat Malt Stout from Scotland. The latter claims to be the only beer in the world to be brewed using malted oats, rather than oatmeal added to the mash.

Above: The characteristic dark, heavy, opaque hue of stout is unmistakable in the glass.

Below: Stout is a derivative of porter. There are many varieties within the general category.

Styles of Beer

Oyster Stout

Stout has always been seen as an ideal accompaniment to a dish of oysters. Some brewers went further and added oysters to their beer. Famous examples from the past include Castletown on the Isle of Man and Young's of Portsmouth in England, who boasted that their oyster stout contained the "equivalent to one oyster in every bottle". The seaport brewers used concentrated oyster extract from New Zealand. Some American and English brewers have occasionally revived the style, but the main bottled oyster stout today from Marston's of Burton-on-Trent contains no oysters.

Russian or Imperial Stout

Originally brewed in London in the 18th century as an extra-strong, export porter for the Baltic, this rich, intense brew with a fruit-cake character was reputed to be a favourite of the Russian Empress Catherine the Great, hence the Russian Imperial title. Many Baltic breweries took up the style, including Koff in Finland, Pripps of Sweden (whose porter was sold under the Carnegie brand name) and Tartu in Estonia.

In England, Courage still produces an occasional Imperial Russian Stout, which is matured for more than a year in the brewery. The nip-size bottles are year-dated, like vintage wines.

TARWEBIER

This is the Flemish word for the Belgian style of wheat beer. See Witbier.

TRAPPIST

Trappist is a strict designation referring only to beers from the five Trappist monastery breweries of Belgium and one in the Netherlands. These silent orders produce a range of strong, rich, top-fermenting ales. The Chimay, Orval, Rochefort, Westmalle and Westvleteren breweries are in Belgium, while Koningshoeven (La Trappe) is Dutch. All the complex, spicy brews are bottle-conditioned. Some number their beers in strength, terming them dubbel or tripel.

Commercial breweries producing ales in the same style, or under licence from the religious communities, have to call their brews abbey beers.

TRIPLE/TRIPEL

These are Flemish or Dutch terms, usually indicating the strongest brew in a range of beers, especially in Trappist or abbey beers. They are hoppy, golden brews, stronger than the darker doubles or dubbels.

Below: The term Trappist is an "appellation". By law only beers produced by the Trappist monasteries can carry this mark.

Urquell

Urquell is the German word meaning "original source". The term should be used to show that the beer is the first or original in its style, such as Pilsner Urquell from the Czech Republic. Often only Ur is used, as in Einbecker Mai-Ur-Bock.

Vienna

The term Vienna indicates the amber-red lagers developed by the Austrian brewing pioneer Anton Dreher, but these beers now have little association with the city. The style is best found today in the Märzen beers of Germany.

Weisse or Weizen

This wheat beer style has grown from almost nothing to a quarter of Bavaria's beer market in 20 years since the early 1970s. The white or wheat beers of Bavaria are made with 50–60% malted wheat. These ghostly pale, often cloudy brews have become a popular summer refresher in Germany. They have the quenching qualities of a lager but, as they are top-fermented, all the flavour of an ale.

This is particularly true in the more popular unfiltered cloudy version containing yeast in suspension, Hefeweizen. Filtered wheat beers are Kristall. Stronger brews are called Weizenbock; dark ones Dunkelweizen. Notable Bavarian wheat beer brewers include Schneider and Erdinger. There is also a stronger Weizenbock at around 6.5% alcohol compared to Weissbier's usual 5%. In north-eastern Germany, a weaker, sourer style made with about half the wheat is Berliner Weisse. Fruit syrups are often added to Berliner Weisse by drinkers to provide a sweet and sour summer refresher. The leading brewers are Kindl and Schultheiss.

Witbier

The white wheat beers of Belgium are also known as "Bières Blanches" in French. These are brewed using around 50% wheat, but then a variety of spices are added, notably orange peel and coriander. This style is also known as tarwebier.

The witbier or bière blanche style has risen like a pale ghost from the dead to haunt every corner of the market, and the best-known example is the pioneering Hoegaarden. When Pieter Celis revived the art of brewing this spiced wheat beer in the small town of Hoegaarden in 1966, he could not have imagined how it would grow. Now many breweries in Belgium and other countries have copied the style.

Hoegaarden is brewed from roughly equal parts of raw wheat and malted barley. The cloudy top-fermented brew differs from German wheat beers through the use of coriander and curaçao (orange peel) to give a spicy, fruity flavour and enticing aroma. Other leading brands include Brugs Tarwebier (Blanche de Bruges) from the Gouden Boom brewery, Dentergems Witbier from Riva, and Du Bocq's Blanche de Namur.

Left: Triple beers are a sub-category of the abbey style.

Above: Hoegaarden is one of the best-known examples of Witbier or bière blanche.

Index

A
Abbey Beers 52
adjuncts 40
alcohol 38, 43
adulterants 41
ale 11, 12, 13, 42, 52
   (see also individual types)
   all-malt beers 40
Alt (Altbier) 23, 52
amber malt 33
aroma 34, 36, 43

B
barley 9, 11, 14, 30-3
   roasted 10, 41
Barley Wine 53
Berliner Weisse 53
Best 53
Bière de Garde 49, 53
Biologique (Biologisch) 55
bio-science 46-7
Bitter 53, 60
Black Beer 53
black malt 33
Bock 53, 54
bottle-conditioned beers 25, 45, 53
bottles 49
bottom-fermentation 13, 16, 38, 39, 42, 43, 57
bragot 56
breweriana 23
brewing 42-51
Brown Ale 53-4
brown malt 33
Burton-on-Trent 29

C
CAMRA 24-5, 60
cans 48, 49, 50-1
caramel 40
caramel malt 33
carapils malt 33
carbonation, artificial 47
carbon dioxide 38, 43, 44-5
cardboard cartons 51
cask-conditioned beers 45
casks 48-9
cherries 27, 40, 41, 57
Chilli Beer 41, 54
chocolate malt 33
clarification 43
colour 16, 27, 28, 40
conditioning 44-5
coopering 48
copper 43
Cream Ale 54
crystal malt 32, 33

D
decoction 42
Diät Pils 54
Doppelbock 54
Dortmunder 54, 55
Double 55
Dry Beer 54
Dunkel 54
Duppel 55

E
Eisbock 53, 55
Export 55, 60

F
Faro 55
fermentation 8, 30, 38-9, 43-4
   secondary 41
   spontaneous 57
Festbiere 58
filtration 45
finings 45
flavour enhancers 41
Framboise (Frambozen) 41, 55, 57
Fruit Beers 40, 41, 55, 57

G
germination 27, 30-1
ginger 27, 41, 55, 60
Ginger Beer 55
Green Beer 44, 55
green malt 31
grist 40, 42
gruit 13
Gueuze 55
Guinness 28, 29, 41, 59, 61

H
heather 10
Heavy 55, 60
Hefe 55
Hell 55°
herbs 13, 41
high-gravity brewing 46
history of brewing 8-25
Hoegaarden 41
Honey Beer 9-10, 41, 55-6
hopback 43
hops 13, 14, 15, 27, 34-7, 43

I
Ice Beer 55, 56
Imperial Stout 56, 62
India Pale Ale (IPA) 56
Ingredients 27-41
infusion 42
Irish Ale 56

K
kieselguhr 45
Kölsch 23, 56
Kriek 40, 41, 57
Kristall 57

L
Lager 13, 16, 17, 28-9, 38, 57, 58

Lambic 55, 57
lauter tun 42, 43
Light 60
Light Ale 57
liquor (water) 28-9, 42
Lite 58
Low Alcohol (LA) beers 58

M
maize 8, 40
maltsters 14, 30-3
malt 10, 11, 14, 27, 30-3, 38
   extracts 41
malt culms 31
malt liquor 58
Märzen 58
mash cooker 42
mashing 27
mash tun 42
maturing 44-5
mechanization 14-15, 31-2, 46-7
Mild 58
Milk Stout 58, 61
monastic brewing 12-13, 16, 34
Münchner 54, 58

N
nitrogen 30, 51, 61

O
oast-houses 27, 36
Oatmeal Stout 58, 61
oats 12, 30, 31, 61
Old Ale 58
Organic Beers 55
Oud Bruin (Old Brown) 58
Oyster Stout 58, 62

P
Pale Ale 56, 58
pale malt 32, 33
pasteurization 47
Pasteur, Louis 38-9, 47
Pils, Diät 54
Pilsner 16, 28-9, 33, 59
Pilsner Urquell 59, 63
popcorn 41
Porter 59, 61
Prohibition 18-20

R
raspberries 41, 55, 57
Rauchbier 59
Real Ale 60
Red Beer 60
refrigeration 17
rice 8, 40
roasting 27
Roggen 60
Root Beer 60
Russian Stout 60, 62
rye 12, 30, 31, 60

S
Saison 60
salt 41
Scotch Ale 60
sediment 49, 55
Sezuen 60
sparging 42
Special 53, 60
spices 13, 41
Steam Beer 60
steeping 30
Steinbier (Stone Beer) 60
Stingo 53
Stone Beer 60
stout 38, 59, 61-2
   (see also individual types)
Styles of beer 52-63
sugar 12, 27, 38, 40
   extraction 30, 42-3
Sweet Stout 61

T
Tarwebier 62
temperance movement 18-20, 60
top-fermentation 38, 39, 43-4, 52, 53, 56
Trappist 49, 62
Triple (Tripel) 62

U
United States 50
Urquell (Ur) 63

V
Vienna 63
Vienna malt 33

W
water (see liquor)
Weisse (Weizen) 63
Weizenbier 57
Weizenbock 63
wheat 9, 10, 11, 12, 30, 31, 62, 63
   torrefied 41
Whey Beer 21
widgets 51
Witbier 62, 63
wood-fired kilns 31
wort 42, 43, 44

Y
yeast 27, 38-9, 47
   wild 57

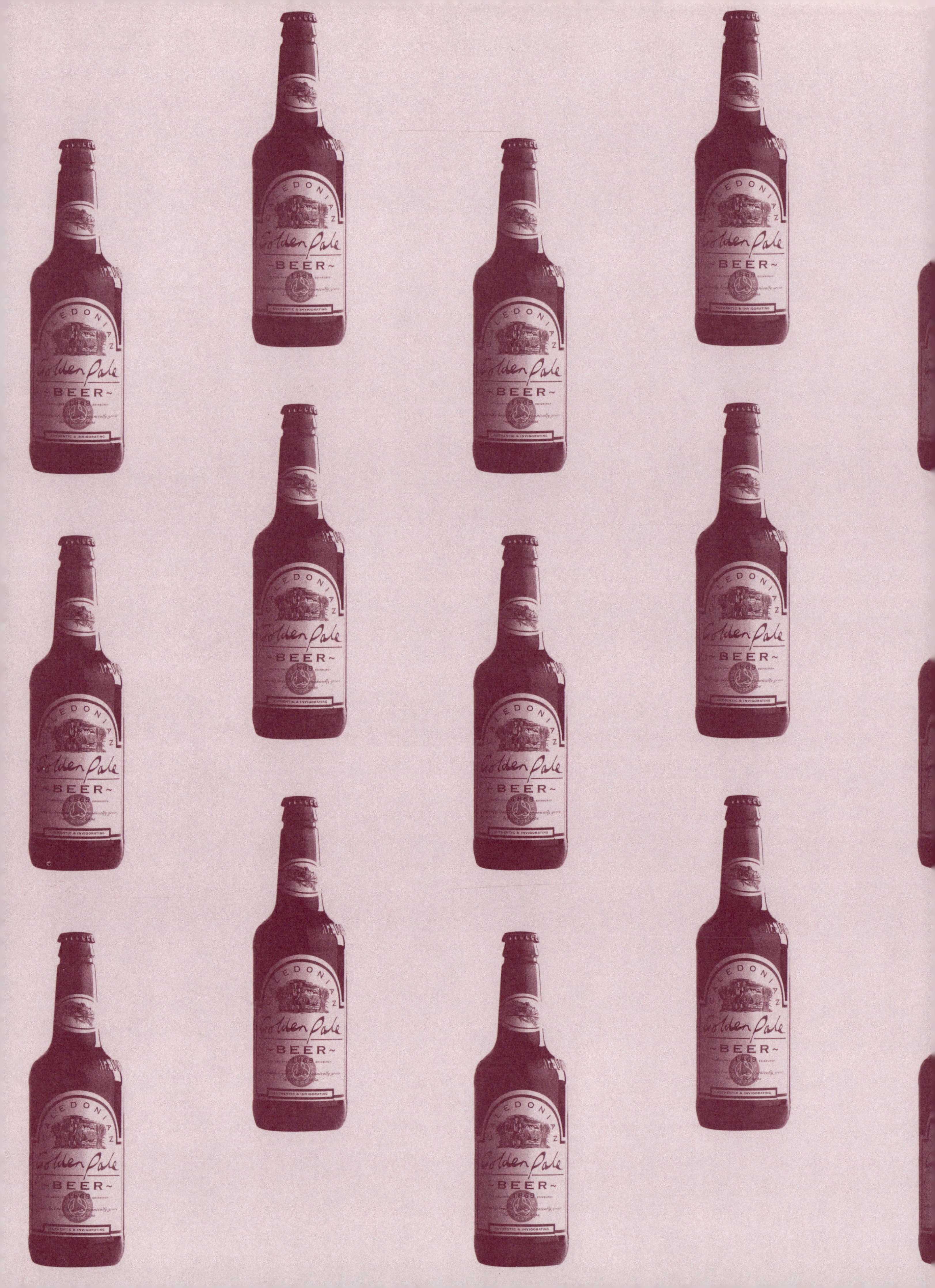
Golden Pale
~BEER~